MW01200944

YOU WANNA BE ON TOP?

YOU WANNA BE ON TOP?

A Memoir of
Makeovers,
Manipulation,
and Not
Becoming
*America's Next
Top Model*

SARAH HARTSHORNE

CROWN
NEW YORK

CROWN

An imprint of the Crown Publishing Group
A division of Penguin Random House LLC
1745 Broadway
New York, NY 10019
crownpublishing.com
penguinrandomhouse.com

Library of Congress Cataloging-in-Publication Data
Names: Hartshorne, Sarah, 1987- author.
Title: You wanna be on top? : a memoir of glamour, manipulation and surviving America's next top model / Sarah Hartshorne.
Other titles: You want to be on top?
Description: First edition. | New York: Crown, 2025. | Includes bibliographical references. | Identifiers: LCCN 2024041587 | ISBN 9780593735244 (hardcover) | ISBN 9780593735251 (ebook)
Subjects: LCSH: Hartshorne, Sarah, 1987- | America's next top model (Television program) | Television personalities—United States—Biography. | Reality television programs—United States. | LCGFT: Autobiographies.
Classification: LCC PN1992.4.H3255 A3 2025 | DDC 791.4302/8092 [B]—dc23/eng/20250113
LC record available at https://lccn.loc.gov/2024041587

Hardcover ISBN 978-0-593-73524-4
Ebook ISBN 978-0-593-73525-1

Editor: Aubrey Martinson | Production editor: Abby Oladipo | Text designer: Aubrey Khan | Production: Heather Williamson | Copy editor: Nancy Tan | Proofreaders: Hilary Roberts and Alisa Garrison | Publicist: Mary Moates | Marketers: Josie McRoberts and Hannah Perrin

Manufactured in the United States of America

9 8 7 6 5 4 3 2 1

First Edition

The authorized representative in the EU for product safety and compliance is Penguin Random House Ireland, Morrison Chambers, 32 Nassau Street, Dublin D02 YH68, Ireland, https://eu-contact.penguin.ie.

For Michael, Meredith,

and, of course, Ian

CONTENTS

YOU WANNA BE ON TOP?

1

I Came Here to Make Friends

"You could be on this show," Michael would always tell me.

"What? No. I've never even had real pictures taken, except, like . . . glamour shots at JCPenney with my mom."

"Sarah, you're tall and beautiful and wild, and your life is even wilder, and I really think they would pick you to be on this show."

"You think I'm *beautiful*?!"

Michael and I met on our very first day at Boston University. My stepdad and mom had decided to divorce the summer before I left for my first semester, so the drive to school was uncomfortable and subdued. When we arrived at Myles Standish Hall, a dorm that had once been a grand hotel, we walked through the lobby, across the aged art deco tile, and rode up in the ancient, creaky elevator to the ninth floor in silence. I'd had to bring everything I owned, since my mom would be moving out right after me, and we carried it up and into my tiny single room, which was barely big enough for the three of us to stand in together. We stood, just a little too close, and stared at one another ruefully as the sound of other families unpacking together rang through the halls.

"Do you want us to help you unpack?" my mom asked.

"No, that's okay. You guys should head home," I said.

We hugged and said some subdued goodbyes. It had been an emotional summer, and there wasn't a lot left to say. After the door closed behind them, I looked around my room, which had probably been built as a closet. It was like nowhere I'd ever been, which was perfect. I loved every inch. The yellowish-white chipped paint on the crown molding that hinted at its grand and storied past. The haunted sounds of the elevator and pipes creaking in the background. The window looking out onto an alley.

As I unpacked, I started to think about the new, better version of myself that I could be now that I lived somewhere where no one knew me. Coming from a small town and graduating from a small high school, in a class of fifteen people, most of whom had known me and every embarrassing thing I'd done since I was eleven years old, the possibilities were endless. Across the hall, I heard my neighbor's mother saying goodbye. I decided this new version of me was brave and walked right into his room.

Sitting on the bed was a petite freshman boy, reading. He looked up from his book, surprised, but didn't flinch.

"Hi," I said. "I'm Sarah."

"Michael," he said. "Hi." His dark eyes wrinkled as he smiled. "Welcome to my room." He had a nasal Jersey accent, kind and sarcastic at the same time. He sounded like a cartoon character; I couldn't wait to hear more.

"Is this your popcorn?"

I maintain that he offered me some, but he insists that I just started eating it. He's probably right. And that was it. We were fast friends.

Sometimes the first friends you make in college are place-holders for the friends you make once you've had time to find people you actually have something in common with. And on the surface, Michael and I were very different. Me, the child of earthy, crunchy hippies from Middle-of-Nowhere, Massachusetts, who grew up without TV or junk food. Him, raised by television and Chef Boyardee in New Jersey. But we're friends to this day.

A few weeks later, I met Meredith in my English literature class. I made a terrible first impression. She and I have a lot in common, except for one important thing. Her focus is like a laser beam, and mine is . . . not. So when I went on a rambling tirade about Gilgamesh, she wrote me off as a bimbo. But we took the same route to our work studies after class, so we started walking together, her thick, long red hair swinging as I grew on her bit by bit until we were best friends. She was homeschooled in New Hampshire and hadn't grown up with much TV either. So I introduced her to Michael, and he introduced us to *Law & Order, Friends,* and *America's Next Top Model,* reveling in giving us our pop culture education. Neither of us had ever seen reality TV before.

"Never?!" cried Michael. "Like . . . none of it?"

It was addicting. There was no writer or director between me and these characters; they were raw and vulnerable, prostrating themselves at the temple of entertainment to be judged not only by the professionals but also by us watching at home, imagining what we would do in their shoes. We watched gleefully as Natasha on Cycle 8 cried on the phone to her boyfriend in the very first episode.

"What a wuss," I crowed, shoving handfuls of Michael's popcorn into my mouth. "They've been gone, what, a day? And she's already crying to her boyfriend?"

We watched as Natasha crooned into the phone. "Do you love me? Do you miss me?" she asked in her thick Russian accent. To this day, when we get on the phone, Michael and I still say that to each other. "Do you loff me? Do you meeeeeeeess me?"

I'D NEVER SEEN anything like *ANTM*. As a kid growing up in a town of 635 people, I obsessed over every glimpse I got into the world of fashion, but there weren't a lot. I read every fashion magazine my school library had. My grandmother saved all her issues of *Elle* magazine for me to read, usually in one sitting, every summer. My parents had a coffee table book called *Of Women and Their Elegance* by Norman Mailer and Milton H. Greene, full of fashion spreads of models and movie stars. I flipped through it over and over and over, wearing down the big, crisp spine, until I'd find my favorite spread: a candid photo of Marilyn Monroe in a light satin dress showing off her pert breasts, laughing with Marlene Dietrich in a dramatic black fur coat and face veil. Two strikingly different examples of glamour: one open and frankly sexual, the other dark and mysterious.

Someday, I thought, *I'll be the type of person who gets to live in the world on these pages. I'll wear designer clothes in my New York City apartment.*

Someday, I'll wear designer heels that won't make my feet bleed, I thought when my pleather heels from Payless dug into my feet at school.

And then that world was seemingly brought to life by *America's Next Top Model*.

"I DON'T KNOW," I told Michael. "I've never even thought about being a model."

That wasn't strictly true. Of course I'd thought about it, but it never seemed like a possibility. I just assumed I was too fat. I didn't know anything about the plus-size industry beyond vaguely recalling the slim sections in the back of my mom's JCPenney and Newport News catalogs filled with smiling, curvy women with gleaming teeth and big, bouncing hair. I'd developed breasts and hips when I was eleven and, with them, abandoned my previous dream of being a ballerina (important to note: I was not good at it).

"It's true," said my dance teacher, sighing as she gazed up and down at my frame. "Modeling and ballet are not for you."

I wore anything from a size six to a fourteen. I'd gained and then lost thirty pounds my freshman year, and those fluctuations, along with my raging body dysmorphia, meant that I had no idea what I looked like. I just knew I didn't look like a model. I knew I didn't look like I was supposed to, like I desperately wanted to.

"I really think you should try out."

"But models are like . . . size two. Size zero."

"Not always! Not on the show!"

He kept at it throughout my freshman year and even found out that auditions were being held in Boston for the next season, Cycle 9, after the summer. I started to consider it.

In the fall of my sophomore year, I met a girl in line for the bathroom at a party, and in the thrall of that particular magic that happens between girls waiting for the bathroom, I sheepishly and drunkenly mentioned that I was thinking about trying out.

"Oh my god, I'm doing it too!" she exclaimed. "You should totally do it, we can do it together, you're so pretty!"

She reached out and caressed my face and ran her fingers gently through my hair. I was completely undone by the sudden compliment. I blushed and wiggled like a happy puppy, almost dropping my Solo cup full of grain alcohol and fruit punch.

"Oh my gosh, no, you are! You look like a real model," I stammered back.

MONTHS WENT BY, and Michael kept telling me to do it. I'd known I was going to do it from the moment he'd first suggested it, but I wanted to seem cool, so I pretended to resist the idea. But that winter, we looked online to find out when auditions started: March 13. It was the day after midterms ended, the day before spring break. It seemed perfect, meant to be.

"DO YOU WANT me to come with you?" offered Michael.

"No, God, no," I said, "but you're an angel for offering." We'd just found out that, although the auditions started at ten a.m., people would start to line up at the crack of dawn.

"But you're going to do it, right?"

"No."

"Sarah!"

"Yes."

In his book *The Wig, the Bitch & the Meltdown*, a novel that pulls angry fistfuls of inspiration from his time as creative director on *Top Model*, Jay Manuel (presumably) took a lot of creative liberties. Despite being there for a small slice of it, I can't really tell what's fact and what's fiction. The one exception is his description of the audition process. I can confirm that his account is completely without exaggeration.

The chapter is called "Cattle Call," which is industry-speak for huge open-call auditions. Most auditions and casting calls are limited to models represented by agencies. But cattle calls are open to the public, meaning anyone from the hopeful masses could be selected.

"The line, no, the *lines* of young women wrapped around the block two, three, four times? Ten thousand girls," remarks a frazzled casting associate character.

The real auditions were held in the center of Boston at the Prudential Center, and I arrived around six in the morning. I hadn't slept all night or for much of the previous week of midterms. I went straight from my professor's office, where I'd handed in my last paper after pulling an all-nighter, and arrived to the Prudential Center to see the longest line I'd ever seen. There were already hundreds of girls sleepily snaking around the building, all the way down Belvidere Street. I slowly, wearily made my way, block after block, to the back. I passed Bathroom Girl partway down. We waved to each other, and I kept on schlepping to the end of the line.

As I took my place, the girl ahead of me shared a rumor that was making its way to the back: they would be admitting only the first five hundred girls, and that didn't include us. The girl's more levelheaded mother chimed in.

"I'm sure that's not true. We'll make it," she reassured us.

More and more girls fed the snake, moving its tail down Boylston Street, creating a spectacle for all the foot traffic. People kept stopping, wondering what was holding the attention of so many young, attractive women: "What are you guys in line for?"

I had fun making up different answers:

"We're shooting a mayonnaise commercial," I'd chirp.

"We're *Jeopardy!* finalists!"

"Reptile People Convention. We're actually covered in scales from the neck down," I said, having just read *Bridget Jones's Diary*.

"No, really," they'd say. "What's happening?"

We'd giggle and demur, but none of us wanted to reveal the truth. I couldn't bring myself to say it out loud, to admit that I thought of myself as hot and interesting enough to be on TV.

We're not supposed to admit we know. That's why we're all obsessed with the origin stories of young actresses and models being discovered in an ice-cream parlor (Lana Turner), a bank (Charlize Theron), an airport (Kate Moss). We love the idea of a pure, virtuous woman who has no idea that she's stunning. And all of us in line that day were breaking the unspoken rule to never suspect it of ourselves. As the day went on, the men started to get hostile toward us.

"Okay, you're all having fun, but seriously now, tell me what's going on," one middle-aged man in an expensive-looking suit demanded, making his way down the line trying to get one of us to crack.

One group of men who'd figured out the truth walked down the line rating us on a scale from one to ten and telling us we would never make it. "Line full of sevens!" they kept yelling. Our rapt attention and desires had nothing to do with them, and that made them furious. That's part of the power of *Top Model:* it's not for men. On the show, I watched the panel criticize girls for posing as though they were in a men's magazine. It might nod to the male gaze, but the show is, ultimately, for the girls and the gays.

Boston had a particularly virulent strain of machismo. Meredith and I, with her curves and voluminous hair and my long legs, attracted a lot of it. Once, a car of men slowed down to follow us as we walked, and when we nervously looked down to avoid their gaze, they screeched away yelling, "You're not even that hot!" Once they were a safe distance away, we burst into peals of laughter. But in the audition line, we didn't even have to wait for them to be a safe distance away. We had safety in numbers. Openly laughing and ignoring them was exhilarating.

Around ten a.m., the line started moving. By that point, I was already delirious from lack of sleep. I did not feel prepared to ask people to put me on TV because I was hot, no matter what random men hanging from the passenger side of their best friend's ride tried to holler at me.

By the time I made it to the entrance of the Prudential Center, the biggest, grayest building in Boston, it might as well have been the gates of Valhalla. Then, slowly, my eyes took in the line ahead of me, continuing to snake into the building, out of sight. I wanted to cry, to lie down right there and just let the rest of the line step over my sleeping body. But another hour or so later, and the actual end *was* in sight. The line went through the building, into the hotel lobby, and all the way to a waiting area outside a ballroom. I'd gotten so tired that everything had started to feel dreamlike, but now this was really happening. I was face-to-face with a real woman, who, I gleefully reminded myself, was involved in making this reality television show: talking to her gave me the second wind I needed. She handed me a clipboard with a questionnaire and directed me to sit in one of the folding chairs nearby. The girl and her mom ahead of me were poring over her questionnaire answers together. I thought about calling my mom. I knew that she would have had some hilarious answers to the questions. I also knew she would never have judged me for being there, but for some reason I was still too embarrassed to call.

I sat outside the double doors of the hotel ballroom on a flimsy folding chair, its legs pushing into plush maroon-and-cream carpeting, and tried to write as small as I could to cram as much info as possible onto page after page. There was a whole section labeled "STRESSES IN YOUR LIFE" in big, bold capital letters, with ten subsections like "family members, such as divorce, illnesses in child or parent, birth or death of loved one" and "with health care services such as insurance benefits, or lack thereof, transportation for treatment, etc." I knew that this was the most important section, the one that would prove whether my life and my struggles were Interesting and Worthy of that ultimate prize: being on television.

Unfortunately, I had no perspective on the stresses in my life. When I arrived at Boston University a year and a half earlier for my freshman year, I thought I had a normal upbringing. But I quickly learned that was not the case. Every time I told what I thought was a funny story about my childhood, I'd watch as people got uncomfortable or, worse, pitied me.

My hallmate and I were talking about riding bikes as kids, and I casually mentioned the women in my dad's apartment building who used to sit on the front porch chain-smoking and making sure all the kids were wearing helmets while they waited for their clients.

"Clients?" she said.

"They were prostitutes," I explained. "Most of the people who lived there were either drug dealers or worked for the drug dealers."

Her face fell, confused. My heart went with it. I loved that building. I loved those women. But immediately I could tell from her expression that, yet again, I'd said something unintentionally off-putting and sad.

"Why did your dad live there?" she asked.

"The rent was cheap, and I guess it was what he could afford," I said, unsure. "And then it burned down." Immediately I regretted letting that slip.

"What?!" she said.

"Yeah, the whole apartment building burned down. On Christmas Day, no less." I chuckled. She didn't. She looked sad. I hated it. I ended the conversation, protective of all the memories I had there.

For the rest of my freshman year, I was an undercover detective, trying to crack the case of what was "normal" without revealing that I was, in fact, not.

To make matters more confusing, most of the other students at BU came from rich families, so they weren't normal either. Growing up, I'd never felt poor. But suddenly, from this new rearview mirror, things looked different. I knew not to talk about things like bounced checks at the grocery store or going on runs to pick up dented cans and other rejected food with my mom. But sometimes things still slipped out.

"Did you hear that Adam is growing mushrooms in his dorm room?" a friend of mine asked.

"Ew," I said. "My dad's roommate used to grow mushrooms, and they smelled *so* gross."

"What?"

"Yeah, something about the spores or the dirt they grow in, it smells musky."

"No, not that. Your dad has roommates?"

Ugh, I thought, bracing myself. I loved all the people who had come and gone throughout the years. Even the terrible ones made for what I thought was a good story, and now I was afraid they were all going to be tainted.

"Yeah, he shares a house with four other people," I said.

"I didn't even know grown-ups could have roommates," she said. "That's so wild. Do they have to share everything? Like the kitchen and the washing machine and stuff?"

"Actually, there is no washing machine."

"What?! How do they do laundry?!" she asked. Her eyes were so wide I thought they'd pop out of her head as I tried to describe the concept of laundromats. But how do you convey that they are the perfect place to read? How do you describe the clanging and humming background noise, the wide variety of people in various stages of washing and drying, pulling their most intimate items in and out of machines alongside one another? How do you explain that orange soda tastes better while you're waiting for your clothes to dry, or how warm they are when you fold them on the yellow table while watching the Spanish soap opera playing on the television mounted to the wall?

Michael, Meredith, and I sometimes felt like an island surrounded by an ocean of rich people.

"I had to literally explain laundromats to a girl yesterday," I griped.

"My roommate's family just, like, has a plane," Michael said. "Like . . . their own plane."

"Jesus, I didn't even know that was a thing."

And now, on this folding chair, my toes digging into the hotel carpeting, I had to be a detective in the opposite direction. I sat there thinking about all the times Michael had said, "Sarah, your life is so weird, they will definitely pick you." All the times people had cocked their heads and said "aww" at me. What had I been talking about? What of all those stories would be interesting enough to get me on television? I had to assume they knew what laundromats were.

I listed every heart-wrenching thing I could think of, displaying all my trauma for them to pick over like a street vendor's wares.

STRESSES IN YOUR LIFE

With housing, such as inadequate housing, homelessness, conflicts with neighbors or landlord, etc.:

My dad and I were homeless when I was in 3rd grade after our house burned down, which sucked. He is always in a fight with his various roommates.

Was it true? Strictly speaking, yes. After our apartment building burned down, my dad didn't have a place of his own for a while. But it was a little slimy of me to use the word "homeless." We had places to stay. But this was the TV version of my life; there was no room for subtleties or gray areas.

I listed my job history and wondered if it would disqualify me. At the time I was working as an administrative assistant at the Boston University Office of Disability and Access Services during the day and a burlesque dancer on nights and weekends. I'd already had a lot of jobs—I've been working since I was eleven. I dutifully wrote down as many as could fit: burlesque dancer, waitress, catering staff, blueberry farmhand, front desk clerk at a country club. I handed in my application nervously. They handed me a sticker with the number 1042 on it and told me to sit and wait some more. I sat, nervously fidgeting. Without thinking about it, I rolled up the sticker with the number on it and then accordioned it back and forth until it was in tatters.

More applicants trickled in and filled out forms until there were maybe a hundred of us sitting and waiting.

"Please put your assigned number sticker on your left arm," someone with a clipboard said.

I looked down at the crumpled piece of trash in my hand and gulped. There was no saving it. I rummaged in my purse, pulled a piece of paper out of my notebook, and wrote the number onto it. *Strike one,* I thought.

We were herded into the hotel ballroom. On the opposite side of the room was a table full of casting associates. They all sprang into motion and spread out across the room as if choreographed.

"Stand next to the wall," they yelled, gesturing and pointing and pulling girls into the room. We all shuffled into line along the edge. There was a piece of tape on the jacquard wallpaper going all around the room, right at eye level.

"Okay, ladies, we need your nose to be touching the back of the head of the girl in front of you," said one of the casting associates, presumably a more senior one because she was shouting instructions from the table instead of darting and herding us around.

"Nose to the back of the head," the shepherding associates started yelling, pushing us closer and closer together.

"Nose to the back of the head" was still echoing throughout the room when I realized with some alarm that I was the only girl whose boobs went past her nose. An associate came up to me to push me as close as my body would allow into the girl in front of me. *Strike two,* I thought.

"Sorry," I said, as my breasts squished into her back.

Finally, there were as many girls in a single-file line snaking around the walls of the ballroom as was physically possible. They closed the door.

"Step out of your shoes!" the woman at the table yelled.

Everyone went to step forward. I was wearing lace-up heeled boots and had to disrupt the line a bit to bend down and get out of them. *Strike three,* I thought, resigned.

I stood back up, and the line rippled a little, then went quiet—shockingly quiet for a room so methodically crammed full of so very many people.

A casting associate walked around the room. Slowly, I realized that anyone who was shorter than the piece of tape was being sent outside. Occasionally they would push down on a girl's hair to double-check that she was tall enough. It was brutal. I couldn't imagine waiting for hours only to be kicked out of the room immediately, shoes in my hand, tape on my arm, tears in my eyes.

Still, it was quiet, except for their footsteps and resigned sniffs.

The woman at the table stood up and started walking around

the room. She called a few numbers as she walked along: "1005, stand over there. 1076, stand next to her."

They walked to where she'd pointed, in the middle of the room and all our sideways stares.

One of the casting associates walked by me and her eyes took me in. "1042, center of the room." My eyes widened, and I walked to the middle of the room. Bathroom Girl was there too. We made eye contact but didn't say anything to break the silence.

They called about twenty numbers and dismissed everyone else. Even then, the room remained eerily silent, except for the shuffling of papers and a few sighs. The only real sound came from the junior associates arranging the selected few into rows spaced out in the middle of the room. Then they started looking at us from all angles, circling and staring. I assumed the breeding studs would be sent in shortly. Of the twenty or so girls, they picked two of us and dismissed the rest. Bathroom Girl waved and shrugged at me as she left. I shrugged back and pulled a face. We laughed silently.

The other girl and I walked toward the table. Somehow, I'd won a gladiator battle without actually touching anyone or making a sound. Had my little blunders made me stand out from the pack? Maybe.

In a society that looks at beauty and fame as the highest accomplishments, it was startling to come face-to-face with how truly arbitrary it all was. Suddenly the girls in line who were trying out for the sixth or seventh time made sense: the selection process was more like a lottery than a competition.

The woman gave us a piece of paper with a time and location on it, a conference room in the same hotel. She told us to come back tomorrow at our assigned time in jeans, a tank top, and high heels (preferably black) and with a bathing suit.

I walked out, past the mélange of girls still waiting, and tried to wrap my head around what had just happened. It was my first audition for anything outside of school.

When I got on the green line train, Bathroom Girl was there. She smiled. I smiled.

"You got a callback," she said.

"Yeah," I said, desperately searching for something self-deprecating to say to cut the tension. But it was five p.m., and I had been in line for eleven hours and awake for thirty-six, so we rode in silence.

I got home and immediately told Michael everything before collapsing and sleeping for a few hours. Later, I stumbled down to meet him for dinner in the dining hall, and we spent the rest of the night crowing over the possibilities.

"You're going to make it. You are going to be on the show."

"No way," I said.

"But what if you do?"

"What if I do?" I squealed. "Maybe I'll be the villain!"

"No," said Michael, "you're too nice."

"Which one will I be then?"

"I don't know. The nice one?"

"The ditzy one?"

He laughed. "Maybe."

Meredith joined us, and I started doing a bit that drove them insane. I had a coat that made me look pregnant, so much so that strangers would ask me how far along I was, and whenever I wore it, I would pretend to be a pregnant teenager from Alabama named Lurlene with a thick Southern drawl. She was looking for the father of her child, whom she'd met and conceived with in the back room of a 7-Eleven, but gosh durn it, she couldn't remember which one! She became part of our lore, and I would become her whenever I wore the coat, whenever we went to 7-Eleven, or just whenever I felt like annoying them.

"I'm gon' be a model, y'all! I bet I get to show off the maternity wear in the Dickies catalog my mama gets!"

"Not Lurlene!" cried Meredith.

It felt like I'd always dreamed college would feel: giggling in bed with friends, making near impossible life plans.

THE NEXT DAY I went back to the hotel at the Prudential Center in my Old Navy outfit and Payless heels and with a bathing suit in my very early 2000s giant purse (from Marshalls, $19.99). I was late, but it didn't seem to matter.

Like yesterday, a handful of casting associates sat behind folding tables covered with papers on one side of the room. On the table in between them was a camera. In front of them was a runway made of plywood that led right up to the camera; it felt as though Tyra Banks were right on the other side of the lens. There was a line of girls all along one side of the room and stretching out the door into the hallway. I gave my name, lingered awkwardly for a while, and then walked to the back of the line. I sat down.

"How long have you been waiting?" I asked the girl in front of me.

"A while. They said they're, like, two hours behind."

I wasn't worried. I came prepared this time: I settled down on the ground with my book and my snack, looking up occasionally as girl after girl went in to tell the casting agents why she, more than anyone, deserved to be on the show. As someone who didn't know if she wanted to model, who tipped the scales at 160 pounds, I had no idea what to say. Luckily, I was given a lot of time to come up with something; I sat there for six hours.

Day turned to night, and we all got silly and punchy. Girls showed off their runway walks up and down the hallway.

"What's everybody's schtick?" asked one girl.

"I was just wondering that!" I said. "I think I'd be the ditzy one."

"That's so silly!" said a girl with piercing blue eyes. "I'd be the beautiful one," she added, flipping her long blond hair over her shoulder.

Maybe, I thought, *I will be the second-most ditzy one.*

"It would be so silly if they didn't bring me into the house," she went on. Frankly, she was right. She did belong there. And who knows if she was projecting confidence or if it was real, but either way, I was so envious. I would have given a pinkie toe to have any sense of confidence or belonging, misguided or not.

First, they put us in groups of ten and had us walk the runway one at a time, then again in our bikinis. I was humbled when we changed into our bikinis and cat walked. *Some of those girls were . . . impeccable. Perfect. Luscious. All that is good,* I wrote in my journal. One of the casting directors asked me to do my walk again.

"Can you do it a little slower and bring a little more confidence? We want to show off all that curvy body."

Oh, you want me to be more confident? I thought. *That makes two of us.*

Finally, it was my turn to be interviewed. I introduced myself and did a little turn for the camera and braced myself. I had an impassioned speech ready to explain why they should still pick me even though I was doing burlesque.

"So, tell us more about the blueberry farm."

"I . . . what?!"

"Tell us what it's like working on the blueberry farm. Is it boring?"

"I mean, yeah, it's super boring. Have you ever been on a farm? It's like that, but we don't get to leave. But, on the plus side, I don't have to pick much anymore because I'm the only one with arms long enough to fix the sorting machine."

They chuckled. "That's great—that's a great detail. Can you say it again, but include the question in your answer?"

Ah, yes, the backbone of all reality television. When you are on a reality show, you spend a lot of time being asked guiding questions about everything that is happening. And, for editing purposes, they need you to paraphrase those questions in your answers so they don't have to include the audio of the producer speaking. They want it to seem like everyone on camera is seamlessly and spontaneously recounting everything without prompting from the person just off camera. So, for example, instead of saying, "Yeah, it's super boring," when I repeated myself, I said, "Working on the blueberry farm is super boring."

"Great, Sarah, thank you so much. So do you like being a simple farm girl on the blueberry farm?"

Without hesitation I said, "Ew, no. I do not like working on the blueberry farm. I don't want to just be a simple farm girl. I want to be so much more than that."

None of that was true. As soon as the words were out of my mouth, I pictured the smiling, bearded face of the kind, older gay man who owned the farm. The warm, cozy inside of his house looked like it was out of a 1970s *Architectural Digest* and smelled like tahini, apple cider vinegar, and soil. I remembered feeling like such a grown-up as I drank my coffee in my travel mug and looked out over the rolling, rocky umber hills. They'd turned that reddish-orange color because the farmers set controlled fires every few years to encourage more fruit growth, a tradition that dated back to before the land was colonized by Europeans.

I'd started working there when I was eleven—my first job. Like any job, it was tedious and frustrating at times, but it wasn't boring. And I never felt like a simple farm girl. The other employees and I were a ragtag group of queer weirdos (although I wasn't out yet) from all over the country, and together we made up a vibrant, eclectic home away from home where I had been able to be my rapidly evolving self every summer for the past eight years. But I didn't say any of that. It wasn't TV ready. Besides, it was working. I could tell that the casting directors liked me.

"And you came here because of a friend, right?"

How the fuck did they know that? I racked my brain, but I didn't think I'd said anything about Michael in my application.

"I . . . yeah. I mean," I said, realizing I hadn't included their question in my response, "I came here because a friend talked me into it." I had no idea what either of us was talking about.

"And your friend didn't get a callback, right? She left in the first round?"

They meant Bathroom Girl, not Michael. When she and I had waved to each other yesterday, I thought we were just peons in a crowd, but they'd been watching us. Spooky. They asked again.

"Can you tell us about how the friend that convinced you to come didn't get a callback?"

"Right . . . yes. A friend talked me into coming and then, well . . . I got a callback and she didn't. Kind of an awkward train ride back to school."

They chuckled.

"Can you tell Tyra what it means to you to be a plus-size model?"

The room started to swim in front of my eyes. I stared into the camera like a deer in headlights. I don't even remember what I said, but it can't have been very good or coherent, because one casting director frowned and looked at me thoughtfully, hand to his chin.

"Okay. Could you maybe say something about why plus-size representation is a good thing?"

"I . . . I think it's important for people to be represented, for them to see themselves on TV, and I think it's okay to be plus-size and, I mean, a model, to model. You should be able to be a model if you're plus-size because then people will see you and feel like they are . . . okay." Well. I'd certainly said . . . something.

The panel of casting directors smiled politely and looked down at their notes.

"Okay, Sarah, to wrap it up, can you tell us more about your time on the blueberry farm? Can you ask Tyra to please save you from a summer of boredom on the farm and make you a top model?"

A lifeline! I was totally picking up what they were putting down: go back to what worked.

"Tyra, if you don't pick me, I will be elbow-deep in blueberries all summer for the ninth summer in a row. Do you know how many blueberry muffins there are in Massachusetts?! *I do.* Please, pick me! Don't send me back to the farm!"

The panel chuckled, and the other girls even looked up and laughed.

Buoyed, I dropped to my knees and wrung my hands. "Please don't send me back to the farm! My fingers can't take another year of being stained!"

As I left, I couldn't believe the blueberry farm was the thing that stuck. Whatever I said must have worked. A casting director called the next day and told me I was making it through to the next round. Mike and Meredith and I all screamed together in my dorm room.

2

Whoever They
Want Me to Be

After the callback, I didn't hear anything for weeks, long enough that I assumed nothing would be happening. Then one afternoon I got a voicemail from a casting associate letting me know I'd made it through to the next level and they'd be checking in periodically over the next few weeks. That I should start getting excited.

"You're going to make it!" said Michael.

"Oh my god, what if I am?!"

And a few weeks after that, they did call.

"I want to talk about your name," said a casting director.

"My name?" I said, unsure if I'd heard them right. I was walking to class across a bridge on Commonwealth Avenue, a busy Boston street.

"Yeah," they said, "do you go by Sarah Hartshorne or Sarah Banks or what?"

My full name is Sarah Banks Hartshorne. Hartshorne is my dad's last name; Banks is my mom's maiden name. I'd been going by "Sarah Banks" for a few years, which my dad was slightly miffed about, but it was easier to spell than "Hartshorne," and I wanted to be Sarah B., like Sarah B. Divine, whose dog-eared biography sat by my bed.

"Sarah Banks," I said, confident I was saying what they wanted to hear. "Hartshorne is my actual last name, but I know it's long, and no one knows how to pronounce it. I go by Banks."

"No," they replied quickly and vehemently. "Let's do Hartshorne. Sarah Banks and Tyra Banks are just way too similar, and you don't want that, right?"

"Right," I said, "yeah, of course. That sounds great." I liked Banks. But I would be whoever they wanted me to be.

And then there was radio silence again. I figured I'd been dropped, until one sunny, unseasonably cold day in May, I got a call from a casting assistant named Lukas who, according to my journal, said without saying that I was on the show, once I passed one (ONE!) more interview, which should be filmed. He didn't have to say. I knew what that meant. I'd seen the grainy home-movie-style clips on the show of a beautiful girl in her bedroom, clutching the phone and sobbing (but make it fashion). "I've always dreamed of being a model!" she'd cry while Tyra beamed, glowing from within by the light of making someone's dream come true.

Lukas got my address to mail me a camera and said they'd call the day after it arrived, sometime between noon and eight p.m. I pulled the package out of my student mailbox and held it like it was the most precious, fragile piece of art, admiring the official casting office return label. I pictured myself grinning and squealing when Tyra told me I would be on the show. I started to rehearse what I would say. *I can't wait! I am going to be America's Next Top Model!*

The next day, when the call came, Mike, Meredith, and I were walking through Kenmore Square to get coffee. Meredith turned on the camera, and we made incredulous eye contact. Was this real? Was I about to be on the phone with Tyra fricking Banks? I was not. I was about to be on the phone with Lukas the casting associate. He told me that, yes, this was real. I was going to be flown out to an undisclosed location for the first episode of Cycle 9 of *America's Next Top Model*. After practicing my reaction so many times, I was just quietly stunned.

"Okay," I said, eerily calm. I didn't feel anything like all those girls I'd seen on the show. "What's next?"

Lukas started on an extensive laundry list of things that needed to be done: "We'll need you to sign the contract, which we'll send you, and there's a form for your doctor to sign and a bunch of other signatures you'll need. You need to erase all of your social media accounts and take down any photos online, but this will all be in the email. And then we need a copy of two forms of ID, including a valid passport. You have a valid passport, right?"

"I do," I said confidently. "Should I still be filming this?"

"Oh," he replied. "No, sorry. You can stop filming."

He continued with the list of things that needed doing. It was a lot of documents, signatures, notarizing, and faxing, which, in my naive youth, felt grown up and exciting.

Eventually, we hung up. Mike and Meredith stared at me, poised and waiting. I looked at them, coming out of the daze. Their excited faces brought me back to reality.

"I'M GONNA BE ON *TOP*!" I yelled.

"Nah nah nah nah nah nah," they sang back, in the tune of the show's signature theme song.

That night, I started to peruse the contract, which was lengthy, to say the least. Right on top was a confidentiality agreement that I read with a tinge of guilt, having unknowingly violated it. Mike, Meredith, and I had told everyone in line at Starbucks, including the disinterested barista, that I was going to be on *America's Next Top Model* (*nah nah nah nah nah nah*). We were undeterred by their indifference. "I'm gonna be a supermodel!" I sang the RuPaul song. Somehow that evolved into all three of us chanting "Inter! National! Supermodel!" much to the chagrin of everyone around us.

Now I realized all that chanting and excitement was in breach of contract. *Oh well. Nothing to do about it now,* I thought. The rest I skimmed, having no idea what most of it meant. I hadn't even thought about whether I would get paid, but I did notice it said that production "could" give us a daily stipend for food but was under no obligation to do so. I checked the dates that were in the email Lukas had sent and was relieved to see they fit perfectly over my summer break. I wouldn't have to pay any rent while I was gone. I was under no delusions that this would make me any money, but I started to get a little nervous about what it was going to cost. I pushed those thoughts to the back of my mind.

The next day I headed to my work-study job at Boston University's Office of Disability and Access Services to use its machines. I watched as page after page (after page after page) of the contract printed out. I initialed page after page (after page after page) and signed at the bottom. I looked askance at the top, which said, "NOTE: DO NOT SIGN THIS DOCUMENT UNLESS YOU HAVE READ, UNDERSTOOD AND AGREED TO IT IN ITS ENTIRETY." Had I read it? Sort of. Had I understood it? Not really. Would I have agreed to anything? Absolutely.

"Is that your passport?!" asked my coworker, interrupting my musings. He was one of those men whose hairline and body were just waiting for middle age so he could assume his final form. His hobbies included listening to his police scanner, collecting figurines, and sexually harassing me. "Can I see it? I bet the picture is hot."

"I was fourteen, so not really," I said, handing it over.

"That's where you're wrong," he said, which was just . . . super chill. "Why do you have your passport at work?"

"I . . . need it for a thing," I said. I was already bad at lying about this. Luckily, he didn't really listen to anything I said.

"Huh. Did you know it's expired?"

"Passports can *expire*?"

The wind had been knocked out of me. My heart was pounding in my chest. I couldn't believe this was happening. I'd been telling everyone it was a silly pipe dream, but in reality, I was desperate for it to come true, and now it was being wrenched away because I was an uneducated hick who didn't know that passports expire. What's next? Licenses expiring?!

I felt panic rising in my throat and shoved it right back down. I decided that this was not going to be the end. I made a copy of my passport, ran to my boss's desk, and grabbed the ink pad she used to stamp our time cards, covered the pad of my thumb in ink, and pressed it over the expiration date on the piece of paper in a giant, smudgy thumbprint. I scanned the doctored copy and sent it off over the fax lines on a wing and a prayer.

I ran back to my dorm room and called my only grown-up friend: the manager of the burlesque troupe I danced with. He looked exactly like the manager of a burlesque troupe should, which is to say, yes, he was a grown man who wore fedoras, but he had the decency to follow through on the aesthetic with wing tip shoes and three-piece suits.

"You know the show I told you about?"

"Yes," he said.

"You need a passport to be on it and my passport has expired. What do I do?"

"Meet me at city hall tomorrow at noon. Bring the contract you just signed and try not to be late," he said. "Everything's going to be okay."

The next day we sat and waited around in uncomfortable government-issue chairs.

"I'd like to give you some advice, if that's all right," my friend asked. His voice was gravelly and deep but still crisp from years of theater training.

"Please," I said.

"I think you'll find that a lot of your relationships are about to change going forward."

"Oh, I don't know," I said. "I don't even know if I'll make it on the show for real. Doesn't it seem like this might just be a silly little anecdote someday?"

"You'd be surprised at how little fame it takes to make people act differently."

"I . . . I don't think this is going to make me famous," I said.

"Maybe not," he replied, "but the goal of this show is to be a famous model, right?"

"Oh God, I guess," I said, wincing in embarrassment.

"If I learned anything from being a child actor, it's that even the illusion of fame is enough. People will think that you can do things for them that you can't really do because they think you have power that you don't really have. Because, you know, you really have no power going into this agreement." He gestured to the contract.

"I know, right?" I laughed. "Totally signing my life away."

"Not your life," said my friend solemnly. "Your life rights."

I DID HOPE this show would make me famous, but I could barely bring myself to be honest in my journal, let alone in conversation:

I am . . . getting ready to film the first episode of America's Next Top Model. *If, for whatever reason, nothing comes of this opportunity, that sentence would not be believed by anybody . . . If this propels me to those places in my dreams, then that sentence captures the moment that started it all.*

Although most people might want it, fame has the lowest odds of success paired with the highest level of shame for those who fail. If somebody changes careers after years as a banker or an insurance salesman, we applaud them. But if you switch careers after working in entertainment, you're a failure. I guess the assumption is that if anyone *could* be famous, they *would*. So, if you stop pursuing it, it must be because you couldn't, and not because you just wanted to do something elsc. When Emily Ratajkowski quit acting, she writes in her book, *My Body,* "most assumed it wasn't by choice. Actors and models couldn't possibly want something else, they figured. Every woman wants to be rich and famous for being desirable."

But while we're all supposed to want to be rich and famous for being desirable, we're simultaneously pressured not to admit it. Just like beautiful girls aren't supposed to know they're beautiful, they're certainly not supposed to acknowledge that they want to be rewarded for it. I was no exception. I was trying to create the illusion that I was just coasting through this experience, that it was just happening *to* me because of some force within me over which I had no control. Because, in a certain light, it felt that way. I had no idea what I was getting into. This was so far outside anything I'd ever experienced or expected. So, I let myself believe that this was just a tidal wave carrying me along without acknowledging all the steps I was taking to get myself there. From where I was sitting, in that uncomfortable chair under the fluorescent lights, clutching a contract I didn't understand, whatever stick was in store was worth that carrot they were dangling: fame.

I was brought out of my reverie by a woman behind the desk calling my name. I rushed up with all my paperwork and hurriedly explained that I needed a new passport within the week.

"Why?" she asked. A totally reasonable question.

"What?"

"Why do you need your passport application expedited?"

I looked at her. I looked at the contract in my hands. I looked at my shoes. "I . . . right. I need it for . . . for . . . travel."

"Yes, I figured as much. Where are you traveling to?"

"I don't know."

"You don't know."

"I do not know. I'm sorry."

"Okay. I do need a reason or a location. Preferably both."

I was drenched in sweat. My friend took the contract from my hand and flipped it open to a page that said *America's Next Top Model* all over it. He handed it to the woman, who looked at it and nodded. I thought she might be impressed, but, God bless her, she kept me humble.

"Fine," she said without a second glance, and stamped my application. "You can pick it up next week."

"I . . . thank you, oh my gosh, thank you so much."

"You're welcome . . . You can go now."

The tired, overworked nurse practitioner who performed my physical at the South Boston health clinic was equally unimpressed when I conspiratorially showed her the form I needed her to fill out and sign. The only thing that gave her pause was how in depth it was.

"Jeez," she said, "they really want to get up in you."

"They really do," I replied, my feet in the stirrups and my eyes on the ceiling. I didn't feel very glamorous or Inter! National!

After the exam, I went back to my room, where my best friend from high school, Maggie, was visiting me for the weekend. I'd thought about trying to lie about what I was doing but didn't have it in me.

"Can you believe this contract?" I told her. "They need my full medical history and the name of, like, every doctor I've ever seen. I don't even know my pediatrician's real name; I just called him Dr. Bob!"

"That is wild," she said, looking at all the paperwork spread over my college-issued composite board desk.

"Will you sign this?" I asked her. "It's the form that will let me talk to you on the phone if I make it on the show."

I sent that same form to my on-again, off-again boyfriend, a few friends, my parents, and my grandfather. Everyone signed, except for my grandfather. We usually talked on the phone every week, but I understood.

"Sarah," he said solemnly, during our semiregular phone date, "have you read this thing?"

"Actually, no, but I read the one I signed. It's pretty intense, I know. I signed my life away."

"Not your life," he said, echoing my friend. "Your life rights. I can't sign over my life rights. I'm a writer. I need those." He chuckled.

"That's fair," I said, and was almost relieved. He was the first person I went to for advice about everything, but I was a little embarrassed to talk to him about this. He was a Serious Writer and Person. Reality television was no place for Serious Writers or People.

But everyone else signed. And everything else got done. I finished all my finals even though I wanted to scribble "I WANNA BE ON TOP" on all of them and slam them on the desk.

I even disabled all my social media accounts and had every photo of me taken down. This was the early days of social media, when everyone still used AIM and MySpace, and Facebook was still only for college students. Every weekend, we would go out, get wasted on jungle juice at the frat houses on Boylston, and take hundreds of nearly identical photos on our digital cameras to prove that we were young, cool, and vibrant. Then on Sunday we'd plug our cameras into our computers and upload all our pictures to Facebook, where they were safe from the prying eyes of our worried parents. I still remember what my mom wrote on my wall the day that Facebook stopped requiring a .edu email address: "WHAT IS IN THOSE SOLO CUPS SARAH CALL ME PLZ."

When I asked all my friends to take down their photos of me, the ones who didn't know about the show were confused.

"Wait, why do I have to take down our photos?" asked one friend.

"I'm just getting off social media for the summer," I said vaguely.

She narrowed her eyes. "Are you going on a reality show?"

"How did you know?!" I gasped, flooded with relief.

"A friend of mine went on an MTV show last summer, and she had to delete all her photos. Which show are you going on?"

I gulped, nervous. What did the contract say about friends who figured it out on their own?

"*America's Next Top Model.*"

"Huh," she said, smiling thoughtfully.

"Oh, I'm, like, the plus-size contestant. I know I'm not, like, a regular model," I said quickly, trying to beat her to the punch. I was sure she was confused because of my weight.

"What?" she said. "No, that's not it. You are so not plus-size. I was just thinking that it makes sense. I mean, you always seemed so glamorous when you trooped into class ten minutes late, dressed to the nines, your hair kind of a mess."

I laughed. "I am hopeless at doing my hair. Maybe they'll teach me."

"Maybe," she said. "Or maybe they'll cut it all off. Anyways, I'll take down the photos. Good luck."

Meredith and Michael had the most pictures of me, of us together.

"Tyra better be grateful I'm doing this," Meredith said as she deleted all online evidence of our friendship.

"I assume she'll send you a thank-you note. Maybe mention you by name in the first episode."

"I mean, it's the least she could do!"

"Do you think you'll be coming back in the fall?" asked Michael. Both of them were staying in Boston over the summer, and I was . . . jealous, which I knew was unfair. But I couldn't help it.

"I don't know," I answered honestly. I wanted to tell them that, yes, of course I would be back as soon as possible, and next year would be just like this year, but I didn't know that. I didn't know if I was coming back. Hell, I didn't even know where I was going: I still didn't know where my upcoming flight was headed.

WHEN MY PLANE ticket arrived in the mail, I learned I'd be headed to San Juan, Puerto Rico.

"What do models wear?" my mom asked, as we looked down at my entire wardrobe strewn across my bed.

"I have no idea," I said. "So far I've packed my pajamas and that's it." I pointed to my most comfortable strawberry-print T-shirt and shorts. Then we picked an outfit for the plane that would be comfortable but still cute.

"When do they start filming? Right at the airport or at the hotel?" she asked.

"I have no idea," I replied. "Should I pack the heels or wear them?"

"Pack them," she said. We agreed: no one wore heels on a plane. We stayed up all night deciding on outfits and speculating wildly.

Before I zipped my suitcase shut, I carefully placed the contract inside, as instructed by Lukas, and assumed that was the last I'd really need to think about it. It was signed, sealed, and faxed—what else was there to say?

3

Shipping In

A few days after arriving in Puerto Rico, I found myself blind-folded and forbidden to speak on a bus full of other young, sweaty, beautiful girls. There are a lot of moments from my time filming *America's Next Top Model* that, looking back, didn't age well. But even at the time, this felt fucking deranged.

It all started when we, a group of about fifty overexcited women, landed in San Juan, flown in from every corner of America. I'm guessing that there were only fifty of us; I don't know if I ever saw all the other girls at once. We were very rarely together in groups larger than four or five, and even then, we weren't ever allowed to speak to one another—which was disconcerting, yes, but we'd arrived! The selected few! Chosen from the boatloads (pardon the nautical pun) of people who had tried out. And now, I was being flown out to Puerto fricking Rico.

As I walked alone through the Luis Muñoz Marín Inter! National! Airport, I felt glamorous, important, and clueless. *"Inter! National! Supermodel!"* I chanted to myself under my breath. It was late May and still cold and gray in Boston. The tropical warmth enveloped me like a humid hug as I walked through the sliding doors outside. Glamorous. Clueless.

Standing in the pickup area of the airport was the most beautiful woman I'd ever seen, in cutoff jeans, a white tank top, and high-heeled Candie's mules, leaning nonchalantly against her Louis Vuitton luggage. I later learned she was Janet Mills, from Bainbridge, Georgia. With a pixie cut and a cigarette in hand, Janet looked like Audrey Hepburn with a tan and a body for days. Next to her was Lisa Jackson, who turned around to face me, and I barely came up to her collarbones, an unusual experience for me, at five foot eleven. I looked up into her catlike green eyes. She smiled down at me. She was also wearing a miraculously unstained white tank top over a denim skirt and espadrilles. I'd never met anyone who wore heels on an airplane before. Lisa was truly stunning: so long and lean and beautiful that I was actually stunned. It was almost jarring, like encountering an alien.

As more and more girls began to gather at our designated pickup spot, they *all* started to look like aliens: impossibly thin, impossibly symmetrical. There was no question what they were there for. I was acutely aware that, on the one hand, they were literally my competition. On the other hand, all I wanted was for them to like me. We'd only just started this insane journey, and already I was desperate for companionship, for one of them to reassure me that this was all out of the ordinary for them too.

"Hi, is this . . . this is . . . is this for the . . . for *Top Model*?" I stammered, my voice cracking.

"Yeah, hi!" said one of the girls.

"Oh, thank *gawwwdddd*," said Janet. "I've been standing here with y'all for twenty minutes too afraid to ask!" Her Southern accent was strong and sweet and punctuated with passionate italic emphasis that really let you savor all the extra syllables. Another girl nearby heard it and asked her where she was from, and they started trading anecdotes about Georgia.

"Where are you from?" someone asked Lisa.

"People always ask that," she replied, "and they can never guess."

"Why, where are you from?"

"Try and guess," said Lisa, addressing us all. I smiled. She was going to do well on the show. She had us in the palm of her hand—we all wanted to be the one who guessed correctly.

"Is it in Asia?"

"Puerto Rican? Are you home right now?"

"Imagine if she's not even here for the show, she just walked by," I said.

"Egyptian?"

"Anyone else?" she asked teasingly. "Jamaica," she said, before proving it with a perfect Jamaican patois. I perked up.

"Oh, I have family in Jamaica. Where on the island are you from?"

Everyone looked at me. I smiled. Maybe I would do well on the show too.

"But how are you Jamaican?" asked Lisa sharply.

I told the abbreviated TV version of events: "No, no, I'm not, but my grandpa took his second wife there, and she liked it so much that she left him for a Jamaican guy," I said, and they all laughed. I felt a little more at ease.

As we sat there getting to know one another, awkwardly and sweetly, the extroverts started to make themselves known. One girl who didn't make it into the house asked everyone to go around and say what they thought their "hook" would be on the show.

"Like, obviously, I'm going to be the sexy Victoria's Secret girl, but what's everyone's, like, thing?" she said.

We all looked around, nervously sizing one another up. Even Lisa looked a little unsure.

"Well, I guess I'll be a Georgia peach with the fat ass!" said Janet, and we all giggled, but I felt a Georgia peach pit in my stomach. This was 2007, the Kardashians weren't famous yet, and a fat ass was not a good thing. If her ass was fat, what was mine?

The whole time we'd been standing there, I'd been clocking the differences between the other girls and myself, and I felt like a whale, thirty to fifty pounds heavier than everyone I could see. I was beginning to realize that I'd been flown out for a different purpose from the other girls. They were all there to compete and prove that they were the Absolute Ideal: what society tells us we are all supposed to aspire to. And I was there to be Almost That but—notably—Not. It was up to me to prove something I wasn't ready to believe: that Not That could be just as good as That.

My body dysmorphia was like a cat, always threatening to knock my dieting off the counter into a full-blown eating disorder, occasionally taking a swing. I had made it a rule never to talk about it ever since I let it slip that I thought of myself as chubby my freshman year. I can still remember my friend's face as she looked at me uncertainly to figure out if I was joking or not.

"Do you mean that?" she asked.

I looked back at her, just as uncertain. I knew I'd said something wrong, but I didn't know what was right.

"I mean, kind of," I said. "I guess maybe that's not the right word, but I don't know."

"Sarah," she said, stern, "it is . . . not the right word."

I felt squirmy, like a grub whose rock has been overturned. My weight and body took up almost all my mental energy, but talking about it seemed to only make it worse. I was tempted to yell, *Pay no attention to that anxious girl behind the curtain!*

And now, as I looked around at all these achingly thin girls, it was starting to hit me that every challenge, every panel, every conversation going forward, was going to be about my weight. That was going to be My Thing, no matter what else I did.

After a few more minutes of chatting, Janet and I retreated, lit cigarettes, and stood for a moment in overwhelmed silence. A crew member arrived in a van and told us to get in.

We arrived at the hotel where we would spend several bizarre, regimented days. The first thing they did was take our IDs, our phones, and our cash. They dropped us off at our rooms and told us to wait for further instructions. I felt more like an Inter! National! Spy! than Supermodel. In my journal I wrote, *It does not seem real. I know I'm sitting on the porch to a beautiful hotel room, waiting for one of the producers to call with instructions. I can hear the ocean, smell the flowers, feel the warm breeze, and see the brightly colored buildings, but it still doesn't seem real. How odd that this should happen to* me. *I keep waiting for someone to come to their senses and realize there's been a mistake.*

Eventually, we got a call from someone who said they were a producer of the show and that a handler would be arriving early the next morning. We would come to spend a lot of time with these handlers, also known as "cast wranglers," which is a job title unique to reality television in that it refers to adults. There are cast wranglers on other sets, but only for children and animals. Most of them were also associate producers or production assistants and had production crew duties in addition to schlepping us around.

For the days we were at the hotel, these wranglers kept us on the move and in small groups. They were mostly recent college grads, new to the industry and chronically overworked. Because they had to be on the move all day long, running after a bunch of confused and hyperactive models, they looked like RAs during finals season: crewnecks, messy hair, and perpetually stressed-out faces. My handler was a girl who had a ponytail that bounced when she was angry.

At seven a.m., she knocked on my door and told me to follow her.

"Hi," I said, trotting after her obediently. "I'm Sarah."

"I know," she said. "I'm Whitney." That was the end of the conversation. She brought me to breakfast with a few other girls, but we were not allowed to talk to one another or anyone. After our muted continental breakfast, they handed out a form for us to sign: "Informed Consent to Psychological Assessment."

"Congratulations on qualifying to become one of the applicants," it read. "I am one of the psychologists and I work for the producers of *America's Next Top Model*." It went on to say that we would be taking "several tests as well as participating in interviews." It urged us to "answer honestly. Remember being 'you' got you here. Think about your answers, but don't linger, obsess, fret, or worry about what is the 'right' answer . . . You should also understand that while you may not wish to participate in the psychological assessment, the failure to do so will preclude your being considered for the show."

All the girls in my group signed. I wondered if anyone refused.

Whitney led all of us into the hotel's ballroom, where a bunch of other girls were already waiting. I was shocked at how many there were: at least fifty. There were folding chairs sitting behind several long tables, all with thin paper booklets and pencils in front of them. As we walked in, I felt like I was filming the CW reboot of high school standardized tests. We were all slightly too old to be high school students, and the hotel ballroom was slightly more glamorous than the auditorium I'd taken the real SAT in two years earlier.

The booklet turned out to be page after page of fill-in-the-blanks personality testing, with questions like "Do you/would you enjoy wrapping an ACE bandage around an ankle?" and "Do you think people are trying to control the way you think?" After I finished, I brought my booklet to the handler sitting by the door. They told me to sit back down and wait until everyone was finished. I wished I had a book or something to keep me entertained and resolved to always keep one on me going forward.

According to my journal, we were at the hotel for three or four days, but it felt like much longer. We rarely saw the producers or anyone other than our handlers. Whoever was in charge were nameless, faceless entities designing our schedules to keep us just slightly on edge at all times. Time got distorted. The wranglers never told us where they were taking us or what was about to happen; they just herded us from room to room, test to test. We put all our trust in these strangers leading us around like very tall children. It was disconcerting but also somehow comforting. Like, yes, I wanted to know where we were going, but it was kind of a relief to just surrender all decision-making and agency for a while.

A small group of us was brought to the hotel lobby, where they told us to sit and wait, before being led away one at a time. I realized with annoyance that I'd forgotten my book in my hotel room again. I read the tourism pamphlets in both Spanish and English and stole a bunch of hotel pens.

After a while, one of the girls whispered, "I think they're taking us to meet with a therapist." I looked up from *Deportes Acuáticos de Aventura en San Juan*.

"No talking," said a handler.

Damn.

We waited a few minutes. The other girls were so visibly on edge that hotel guests started to avoid walking too near us.

"My parents will be *so* mad if they find out I talked to a therapist."

"So will my boyfriend!"

My eyes bugged out of my head. I wanted to tell them those were actually both *great* reasons to see a therapist.

"No talking," repeated our handler.

Finally, it was my turn. I was excited. I like therapy. The handler walked me into the room, which, despite being in the middle of a hotel, looked like a TV set of a psychologist's office: bland decor, an armchair, a desk covered in assorted papers, a leather couch. Did the hotel rent out offices? Or had the producers rented furniture to convert the room? Where was the bed? I didn't know if we were allowed to ask those kinds of questions. The therapist also looked like television's idea of a therapist. He sat in the armchair, peering over thick, chic glasses with thoughtful, tastefully Botoxed eyes. How does one become the psychiatrist for a reality show? What was the rest of his life like? His voice was warm and authoritative in that particular therapist way.

"Have a seat," he said, gesturing at the couch.

I sat down and smiled at him. Suddenly I was nervous. I realized this was not like any therapist I'd ever spoken to before. I had no idea what was expected of me or what I was supposed to do or say. He and I might be the only ones in the room, but I could feel the presence of the producers he would be reporting to later. This was, in reality, a performance.

He looked at his clipboard. "I have to be honest: I've never seen a personality profile quite like this before."

"I . . . oh. Sorry? Or . . . thank you?" All I wanted and feared most was male attention, and here it was. He smiled a vague smile. I smiled back, unsure.

"Can I ask why you answered yes to the question about whether people are trying to control your thoughts?"

I told him that between advertisements, the internet, social media, and television shows, there were a lot of people spending a lot of money to get all of us to think certain ways. He smiled again and made a note. I didn't mention the people who had flown me to Puerto Rico, put me up in a hotel, and sat me down in this room with him, but I was pretty sure they wanted me to think a certain way too.

After meeting with the psychiatrist, I came out and saw Whitney waiting for me. She looked frazzled and was impatient to shepherd me to our next unknown location.

"Could I use the bathroom?" I asked.

"No," she said, which was not the answer I expected.

"But . . . I have to pee."

"You can pee once we get there. We're just going across the hotel."

"I'm so sorry, but I don't think I can hold it that long. I really, really have to go."

She sighed and took me to the nearest bathroom. Afterward we walked for a long time in awkward silence, her ponytail bouncing. She was annoyed. I was confused and annoyed. We walked down the hall and across a beautiful outdoor courtyard, took the elevator up, and went down another long hallway. It was a long enough walk that I felt validated.

"I definitely would not have been able to hold it this long, if that helps," I said with a little laugh.

"I mean, yeah, okay," she said coldly, and knocked on the door. A young woman in a lab coat opened the door with a big smile and handed me a cup.

"Welcome! This is for a urine sample; can you head to the bathroom behind me?"

"Aha," I said, taking the cup. I went to look back at Whitney, but she had already slammed the door behind her.

I smiled back at the woman and tried to explain that I could not, in fact, pee into this cup.

"Well, just go into the bathroom and try," she said.

I sat in the hotel bathroom and tried in vain, running the water and shifting back and forth on the toilet seat. Once again, my body was getting in the way of my desire to make these people happy. They said not to worry, we would try again later (they never did), and in the meantime, they were just going to draw some blood.

When I get blood drawn now, I know to warn them that I'm prone to fainting, to eat a piece of candy to counteract the blood sugar dip, and to try to breathe through it. But back then I just tried to muscle through it before suddenly turning gray and keeling over, shocking the poor nurses, who had no idea until I hit the ground. And the woman in that converted Ramada hotel room was, sure enough, totally thrown when my hands went limp and my eyes and then head started to roll back.

"Oh my god!" she cried.

I tried to say, *I'm sorry*, but it came out slurred and weak: "Sssssurry."

I ended up on the floor sipping some juice while she sat in the corner and took deep breaths. A man in a lab coat, who I assumed was a doctor, reassured us both that we were going to be fine.

"The hard part's over," he said, helping me off the ground. "Now go change into this gown and hop up on that table."

I took my clothes off and pulled on the flimsy paper gown, which barely covered my ass. I stared at my ashen, sweaty face in the mirror. *You got this, Sarah. You can still salvage this. Just be on your best behavior for the rest of the exam, and you can get out of this with your dignity intact.* I splashed some cold water on my face, walked outside, and jumped up on the exam table with a smile.

The moment my butt made contact with the metal table, I heard a tearing sound as the model-sized dressing gown burst open and tore down the front. I sat there, maintaining surprisingly confident eye contact for a girl whose breasts were flapping akimbo in the wind. I cleared my throat. "This does not fit."

Without a word, the doctor handed me another gown to wrap around my top half before he did a brief exam, checking vitals, listening to my heartbeat, and taking a hair sample.

Afterward, a handful of other girls and I were sitting outside the "doctor's office." It was a rare moment of calm, and we even got to talk to one another a little.

"How'd it go in there?" asked one girl who hadn't been in yet.

"It was okay, but I had just peed, so I couldn't go in the cup," said another.

"Me too!" said another.

"Me three!" I said, so relieved. "And I almost fainted, *and* the gown totally ripped down the front when I put it on. Just . . . tits out."

"Oh my god," they said, putting their hands in front of their mouths, scandalized and sympathetic.

"Stop. You make me giggle," said a girl with the most beautiful smile I'd ever seen.

A girl named Michelle hesitantly asked everyone, "Do you know what they were testing for?"

We all shook our heads no.

"Drugs, probably, right?" she said.

We all nodded our heads in agreement.

"I know that when they take the hair like that, they're checking for weed, and they can detect if you've gotten high in the last, like, three weeks or something," said another girl.

We all nodded sagely. This was right after Britney Spears had shaved her head, and there'd been a lot of speculation that she'd done it to avoid that exact test. There was silence again.

Finally, another girl spoke up. "Okay, I . . . I have definitely gotten high in the last three weeks."

The second the words were out of her mouth, none of us were strangers anymore. We were coconspirators huddling together, navigating the chaos around us. It was such a release, the confessions poured out like water.

"Girl, I've gotten high in the last three *days*."

"I'm pretty sure I still have ecstasy in my system."

"Oh my gosh, me too! Fun!"

"I wish I could get high here!"

"How long do mushrooms stay in your system?"

"Are they going to kick us off when they find out?"

"I have no idea! Can they call the cops? Was it in that contract we signed?"

"I have no idea; I didn't read it."

"Girl, don't sign shit without reading it!"

"I didn't read it either! It was, like, a million pages long!"

It felt so good to finally be talking about how stressful and surreal this whole situation was after rattling around in a cone of silence for so long.

Eventually, the forces that be whittled us down to the thirty-three girls who would make it on camera for the first episode. I think about the girls who were sent home a lot. Were they told why they were disqualified? Did they get to talk to one another on their way home? Were their wranglers kind? What did they tell their friends and family? Had they celebrated with friends like I had? Or had they been savvier than I and kept it a secret like they were supposed to?

They told the remaining thirty-three that filming would start first thing the next day. It was a relief, being in my room and having something concrete to look forward to. I felt more rooted in time and space. Sure enough, bright and early the following morning began the weirdest day of my life. And this is after giving blood and flashing my tits in a Puerto Rican hotel room.

After breakfast, we were herded into the parking lot, where, according to my journal, we stood, caught sight of a camera, and gasped with relief at being allowed to talk. They filed us onto a tour bus. Once we were all seated and the camera crew was settled, we all excitedly bellowed our introductions as a tour guide named Greg marched confidently onto the bus. Greg's vibe was the student who reminds the teacher to give homework over the weekend. Now he had the impossible task of getting thirty-three anxious, flighty girls to pay attention to a dry lecture about the history and architecture of San Juan after they'd been kept in almost total silence for days.

He never stood a chance. *Who wants to listen to Greg talk about the capital when we can finally SPEAK!!!!!* I wrote. Oh, Greg.

But all our eyes swiveled right to him at the end of the tour when he asked us to put on the blindfold that was, apparently, under our seat. The camera crew prowled up and down the center aisle of the bus capturing us dutifully putting them over our eyes. They even tested a few girls by waving in their faces. The bus trundled over miles of unseen narrow, winding Puerto Rican roads. Every time I peeked beyond the blindfold, I saw more girls turning green. I had never been more grateful for my iron stomach.

Finally, the bus stopped. If you watch the episode, it looks like we got off right away, but in reality, we had to sit blindfolded on the bus for what felt like hours while they set up the cameras outside to capture our surprised reaction. Every few minutes they told us, "Just a few more minutes!"

I wrote, *We were so naive then. We actually believed it would only be a few minutes. Forty-five minutes later we'd traversed the bus, a parking lot, a flight of stairs, still blindfolded!*

As I stood there, blind and mute on the hot pavement, no idea where we were, I wondered what my dad would think.

If only we'd paid more attention to the tour guide, I thought ruefully.

Cloth still over our eyes and hearts in our throats, the sudden booming voice of Miss J, runway coach diva extraordinaire and *Top Model* judge, rang out around us: "Take off your blindfolds!"

As I pulled mine off, she was a sight for sore eyes. He's tall, around six foot five, and effortlessly chic, defying gender and fashion norms with a flick of the wrist. *Tall, glamorous, and smarter than us,* I gushed in my journal. I had loved watching him on earlier cycles when he would teach the girls how to walk the runway, cutting them down with just the right insult and then building them back up into supermodels. And now here she was, in the flesh. Our casual summer outfits paled in comparison to his chic ensemble. His skin glowed against a white headscarf casually wrapped around their hair. We blinked and grinned at him as we tried to get our bearings after that blindfolded bus ride.

"Good afternoon!" he said. Was it afternoon? We had no way of knowing, but it was hot.

A glimmering, beautiful cruise ship rose up behind her. "Girls, this is your home for the next week."

We were all, of course, supposed to react as though this were the most marvelous thing we'd ever heard, which, to be fair, was almost true.

I had no memory of the blindfolds or seeing the cruise ship for the first time. It was shocking to see them while rewatching the episode and even more shocking to find that I'd written about them in my journal at the time. I remember the days leading up to being filmed clear as day, but when the cameras turned on, things get blurrier. Jia Tolentino writes about a similar experience during her time as a reality TV contestant in *Trick Mirror:* "I was amazed, watching the show, to see how much I had forgotten. There were entire challenges I had no memory of . . . I forget everything that I don't need to turn into a story." Just a year earlier, I'd been in awe of how raw and exposed reality TV contestants were from the safety of Michael's dorm room, and now I was opening myself up to those same vulnerabilities. It was the producers who would tell my story now, not me. Tolentino writes, "Making sense of what happened every day was someone else's job."

All memories are unreliable, including and maybe especially mine. Entire years of my life are blurry in the rearview mirror because of post-traumatic stress disorder. Some come back, bit by bit, in brief flashes, like glimpses of the night in car headlights driving at great speed. When I hear most people talk about their childhoods, it feels like they have videos, where I have photos and GIFs. How fitting, then, that one of the major events of my life should be a reality TV show (about being photographed, no less).

But there is one moment that has, somehow, stayed fresh in my memories. Miss J did a "fashion inspection" where they went through our suitcases and threw away all the clothes that he didn't like before giving us a "boarding pass" to get on the ship. A few feet away, off screen, a PA stood with our real boarding passes.

Miss J hated everything in my suitcase. My pajama shirt with little strawberries all over it: in the trash bin. "I swear I never wear that in public, just to sleep," I joked, hoping that would keep it from getting thrown out. All my pants: in the trash. In her defense, they were all low-rise bootcuts with pre-worn holes in them. In *my* defense, those were in style back then. But every-thing got chucked except for a dress from my step-grandmother Chase (who is still one of the best-dressed people I know): a black-and-white patterned dress with a Sabrina neckline. "*This* is the kind of thing you should be wearing; this suits your frame," he said, with her signature emphatic diction. I was trying to smile and be game for anything while staying properly humbled. My clothes suddenly looked so basic under her discerning eye. She was a perfect, shiny key to the world I'd pored over as a kid. Still, I wished my clothes weren't all in the trash, even if they were basic.

"If they throw away my shoes, I'm gonna die," said one girl. They edited out the part where she said she couldn't afford to replace them.

Afterward, the PAs handed each of us the trash bag that Miss J had thrown our clothes into. We silently pulled every-thing out and repacked it, sweating and subdued under the hot sun. This moment didn't make it into the episode, of course.

After the "fashion inspection," we changed into the outfits Miss J chose for us and waited around some more. I don't know if it was stress, dehydration, or standing for hours on a hot ce-ment dock, but suddenly I felt like I was going to throw up. My iron stomach was rusting after all. I was terrified of making a fuss, but I walked over to a crew member and told them as casu-ally as I could. "Sorry, I can't take you to the bathroom right now; we have to stay in sight," she informed me, before taking me a few feet away. She seemed unfazed as she watched me retch on the pavement *rather neatly and quietly,* according to my journal.

"Don't worry," she told me as we walked back. "It literally hap-pens all the time. You're not even the first today, I don't think."

I don't even remember which crew member it was. I doubt she remembers me. This was the ninth season, or cycle, of the show, and the contestants must have blurred together after a while. Everyone on the crew was nice enough, but each passing moment was more important to us than it was to them, which made them seem powerful and aloof even when they were being kind. This was a once-in-a-lifetime opportunity for us. It was a day job for them. Most of them had moved to LA to work in movies or scripted shows, and reality shows were just a waystation.

Afterward, I felt better. Cold, clammy sweat seeped through my thin jersey dress as we walked back to the group like nothing had happened.

I got in line to get my picture taken for the "boarding pass," the first photo challenge. All the other girls looked like they knew exactly what they were doing. I studied their every move, praying that by the time I got there I'd know what to do. The photographer took one shot, and it went so fast I barely even noticed it. I walked away, dazed. I told myself that, at the very least, I probably didn't look like I'd just been throwing up in a parking lot.

"Yes, girl, you look fierce in that dress," said Miss J. She was being kind and it made me want to cry.

Boarding the ship took hours. We sat with our luggage, and one by one someone gave us our IDs to present to the confused cruise ship staff and then immediately took them back. Once we made it through, our luggage disappeared, and we trotted after Miss J for a tour of the ship, which was obviously an advertisement for the cruise company. "There's a rock-climbing wall, two swimming pools, two hot tubs, an ice-skating rink, a casino, and a plethora of stores," said Miss J, gesturing like a flight attendant.

As the ship sailed away from port, I was surprised to spot the production crew in a speedboat zooming at a breakneck speed alongside us filming the ship. "Whoa," I said, pointing.

"No talking," said a crew member.

After so many months of waiting and wondering, I was finally in the thick of shooting the first episode, and it all still felt confusing and opaque. Like a party in a dream where everyone knows more than you do, and also there are some random celebrities milling about.

At the end of the tour came our first challenge: a "fashion show" where we were to walk up and down the deck in bulky life jackets. Miss J said, "You've all seen models walking the runway. Now, it's your turn."

My life jacket, which smelled like chlorine and stale body odor, covered my ears completely, coating the sound of Miss J's voice and the crowd milling about in the background with a gentle *whoosh whoosh*. I realized in an alarming flash that, in fact, the only models I'd ever seen walking down the runway were . . . other *Top Model* contestants, while watching the show. I'd never seen a real fashion show before, just pictures in magazines. They'd picked me to be on the show precisely because I had grown up in a town of 635 people with no TV, but suddenly, standing on the deck trying to figure out how to do a runway walk for the first time in my life, I realized that didn't mean it was an advantage.

Oh well, I thought, and tried to strut. *Whoosh whoosh* went the life jacket.

"Boring!" yelled Miss J.

I tried harder, pointing my toes and swishing my hips.

"Better!"

Whoosh whoosh.

They had to edit this scene around the yells and jeers from the regular passengers around us, who apparently did not know they had signed up to be extras on a reality show and were not happy about it. A Pixar cartoon of a grandmother in a floral skirted swimsuit screamed in my face, "I came all the way from Idaho, and you *bitches* ruined my vacation!" before spitting at us. The crew hurried us inside.

Later in the day, I found myself next to Miss J at a quiet moment. I racked my brain for something to say, but I didn't know anything about him. I didn't know anything about all the stories they must have had about supermodels and New York and Paris, oh my. I just knew that I desperately wanted to be close to him. So I thanked him for picking the dress. "It's a nice dress," she said sweetly, considering the haute couture that filled his life when they were not responsible for hordes of awkward, birdlike girls.

MUCH LIKE THOSE in the hotel, we spent our five days on the ship completely cut off from space and time, even more so given we were literally at sea. They'd tell us what to wear and bring, but we never knew if we were going to the dining room for lunch or one of a seemingly infinite number of conference rooms to sign contracts or simply sit for hours with no explanation.

We always hoped it was the dining room. Mealtimes were the only times we were allowed to talk and look out the windows.

One morning, they filed us into a different room for breakfast. It was a low-ceilinged, dimly lit, windowless room with café tables surrounding a small, shoddy stage dressed up with velvet curtains like at a comedy club.

A bunch of girls turned green from the rocking of the ship in the darkness. The rest of us nibbled on our food and waited in silence. I'd eaten bacon off three other girls' plates by the time a producer finally told us that something was about to happen— and we had to absolutely scream our hearts out when it did.

There she was: Tyra. Stunning, six feet tall, dressed like a couture showgirl, surrounded by a team of beautiful men all dancing behind her in sailors' outfits that looked like they came from Shein. She was singing a song, but we were told to scream through it, which we did again and again and again. We did four or five takes, screaming at the top of our lungs, completely drowning her out every time. I assumed it would sound better when the episode aired (it didn't).

Finally, Tyra smiled and gestured for us to be quiet. And in that distinctive, authoritative voice, she told us, "Today you will meet with the panel of judges, and we will decide which of you will go on to become America's! Next! Top! Model!!!"

An hour later, they divided us into groups of six and led us to a stairwell. A sound guy came and strapped a mic pack around my waist and fed the mic cord up my shirt. While he was clipping it to my bra, a producer asked me, "What's your talent?" Seeing my face go blank, he offered by explanation, "That girl is rapping, that one is singing a song, that one wrote a poem."

If society had taught me anything, it was that I should be able to coast on my looks, and here I was, on a reality show about being pretty, and that wasn't the case?!

My cruise ship bunkmate, Ebony Morgan, said, "Why don't you do that thing that you did at dinner the other night?"

"Ask if anyone has an eating disorder?"

"No, girl," she said, giggling. "That's what I did. I meant the thing with the paper straw up your nose."

"Oh, right," I said, laughing a little.

The producer's ears perked up. "What thing?" he asked, his eyes narrowing like a cat stalking its prey.

"Oh, it's a silly thing my great-grandmother taught me. It's, like, a bar trick."

"Perfect," he said. "Do it."

It wasn't a good plan, but it was a plan. I took a strip of paper, accordion folded it into a tiny ball, and shoved it up my nose.

"Listen, the judges aren't going to react to whatever you do, so don't worry if it's awkward," said the handler, casually warning me about my worst nightmare before shoving me out onto the stage. I walked out into the spotlight, the three judges in front of me in a cavernous theater and otherwise empty front row. Tyra was in the middle, Miss J on one side of her and Mr. Jay on the other. Mr. Jay was the creative director, so normally his job was to coach the models during photo shoots, but for the first episode, he got to sit at the judges' table and help decide which of us would go forward. His icy gray hair shined in the lights, perfectly framing his perfect face. The three of them looked tiny in the empty auditorium, but my tunnel vision couldn't see anything else.

I smiled and tilted my head up so they could see the contents of my nostril.

"Uh-oh, what happened? Did one of the girls punch you?" asked Mr. Jay.

"Oh, do I have something in my nose? How embarrassing," I said. I pulled the accordioned paper out to silence, as predicted. I introduced myself and answered their questions, which ranged from the generic "Tell us about yourself" to the slightly more intrusive "Is it hard being bigger than all the other girls?"

In the days after the panel, we spent most of our time in cruise ship conference rooms. "Cruise ship conference room": what a grim phrase.

The only way to get some fresh air was, ironically, to go smoke a cigarette. And the person in charge of taking us outside was the very visibly pregnant supervising talent producer, Michelle Mock-Falcon. We'd urge her to step away or stand downwind, all to no avail. Why was she the one taking us? How could she stand to be on a boat surrounded by cranky, chain-smoking models?

It was on one of these cigarette breaks that I finally got to meet and talk to the only other plus-size girl who made it onto the boat, Tara. She was stunning: long red hair, big blue angelic eyes, and porcelain skin with the kind of freckles I see girls desperately trying to re-create in makeup tutorials. We'd been eyeing each other for days, and talking to her felt like a port in the storm. She'd actually modeled before the show, she told me. My eyes lit up. A real live plus-size model! I started peppering her with questions.

"Is there any point in even doing runway?" I asked.

"I mean, I think I have a pretty good walk," she said, surprising me. "And there are a few plus-size girls that do walk in fashion week. It's competitive, but not impossible."

I'd never heard of fashion week, but I smiled gamely and kept asking questions a mile a minute.

"I'm sorry, thank you so much for telling me all this," I said.

"Hey, us curvy girls have to stick together," she said, smiling. Her teeth were perfect. I ran my tongue over my own and felt how crooked they were. "After all, we're going to have to work twice as hard if we want to make it."

Her words stuck with me. I was going to have to work twice as hard as these girls at something I didn't understand.

The ship made several stops at various islands, but we would never have known that from inside the conference rooms. Until we stopped at Saint John's on Antigua, where they led us off the boat, blinking in the sunlight. It wasn't just our first time off the ship; it was our first time outside in days.

They loaded us into a van, and I ended up talking to a girl named Kimberly Leemans, bonding over a love of dogs.

"I had the best dog. I think my dog dying was, like . . . the most traumatic thing that ever happened to me," she said.

"Oh my gosh, me too!" I said.

"Yeah, I just had such a good childhood that that's, like, the only bad thing that ever happened to me."

"Oh," I said, giggling a little at the disconnect. "I had a pretty messed up childhood. A bunch of stuff happened. I just really loved my dog. Her name was Shucks!"

"That is an amazing name," Kimberly said, beaming at me with her toothpaste commercial smile. "I love it."

"Like what kind of bad stuff?" asked another girl, with a glint in her eye that made me uncomfortable. I had been in front of the camera for only a few minutes, and I wasn't ready to perform.

"I put it all on the application," I said. "Nothing that interesting."

THE EXCITEMENT IN the van was mounting. We giggled, shouted, and danced with excitement, as Mr. Jay and Miss J poked their heads in.

"Guess what, y'all?" Mr. Jay asked. "We're taking you to the beach!"

We all screamed. Mr. Jay struggled to conceal an eye roll. Miss J blew us kisses.

They drove us to a beautiful tropical beach where we saw Jaslene, winner of Cycle 8, posing for a photographer in the water. *It looks like a TV set*, I thought, before remembering that it was. We ran toward her, screaming as instructed. She kicked her foot in the water playfully and hugged Mr. Jay and Miss J like old friends.

"Tell us," asked Mr. Jay, his arm wrapped around her, "what has it been like being a top model, truly?"

"Oh my god, I feel like the luckiest girl in the world," she said, grinning, "and I worked really, really, really hard, and traveling here and there—"

"Booking covers, working!" interjected Mr. Jay. "And now it's time for your photo shoot," he said to us.

We all stripped down to our bathing suits, and they took us one by one into the water, where we got five shots to get a good picture. For context, at a typical photo shoot, a photographer will take hundreds of shots, so there was a lot of pressure to get it right. While each girl was shooting, the rest of us lounged, swam, frolicked, and drank sodas on the idyllic beach and under cabanas.

Marvita, a stunning woman with a six-pack and a faux-hawk, started running up and down the beach.

"Damn, Marvita," I yelled. "You're making us all look bad! You're going to cause a riot with that body!"

We were still heavily supervised, but I felt so free and relaxed. It was the first time in almost a week that we were able to just get up and go to the bathroom or to get some water without having to ask permission.

Back at the dock, Mr. Jay asked us, "Did you girls have fun?"

"Yes!" we screamed with reckless abandon, as instructed.

"Well, for some of you, the fun is over," said Miss J.

I had to stifle a laugh. I'd never heard someone talk like that in real life. Thirteen of us were about to be left behind in Saint John's. Mr. Jay and Miss J urged us to run as fast as we could to the twenty boarding passes to ramp up the excitement, but I walked over slowly. I was tired from the sun and sure that my picture wouldn't be there.

But then . . . there it was. The photo of me taken right after I'd nearly thrown up on my handler's shoes. I couldn't believe that was only five days ago. My hair was windblown across my face, nonchalant but intense. I was so proud that I could look so good while feeling so bad. I looked like a model. It was an addictive feeling. Maybe I wasn't as out of place as I thought.

Those of us with boarding passes got back on the ship, and the camera crew had us lean over the edge of the deck and wave goodbye at the cluster of heartbroken girls on the dock.

"Wave harder!" the director said. "Blow kisses!"

The dock girls all waved back up at us, presumably instructed to do so by the crew filming them down on the dock.

I felt like an asshole, like I was mocking girls I'd spent the last five days trauma bonding with. I wanted to go hug them, to tell them the process was totally random, but there was nowhere to go but back out to sea.

4

The Contract

Before boarding the cruise ship SS *Adventure*, the contract the show had sent me seemed huge. There were hundreds of pages of legalese that I barely understood. But by the time we docked in Saint Martin, it felt like an albatross.

A few days in, the shine had worn off a little, and the show started to feel like a cult, from the undisclosed filming locations in international waters to not being allowed to speak for days at a time. The language that they hammered into us over and over again urged us to be grateful for this opportunity. And the reality is . . . it *was* a cult. I got suckered into a cult.

Negotiating never even occurred to me. But if it had, all the lawyers I interviewed for this book agreed: *It's not an option. Either you sign or you don't. You're in or you're out.* "You are not going to get control over how you are represented" under any circumstances, said one lawyer. And yet we all signed it. I didn't care how I was represented as long as I was represented on TV.

EARLY IN THE morning on our first full day aboard the cruise ship, we were led into some kind of conference room and told to wait for five minutes, which turned into hours. The room was hotel fancy: a lot of shiny fake wood paneling and inoffensive carpeting. It was a stark visual contrast to our tropical cruise wear: jean shorts, espadrilles, and spaghetti strap tank tops. We shivered in the harsh air-conditioning. There weren't enough chairs, so some of us sat on the ground. We started upright and alert, trying to blend into the professional-looking background, but as the minutes dragged on, we slowly drooped and slouched toward the ground like neglected houseplants. Finally, a team of mostly men and a few women barged through the door. Their suits and intense businesslike energy sliced through the air. They were like vaguely corporate alien invaders to our lush, listless planet.

They introduced themselves, but I couldn't pick any of them out of a lineup. They were just so . . . grown up, and I felt like a child sitting crisscross applesauce on the ground and staring up at them, patiently and nervously waiting. There were lawyers from the production company and executive producers. They were the top of the production pecking order; everyone else in the crew deferred to them.

They began a group presentation that was clearly well rehearsed. One would speak and then seamlessly cede the floor to another. After all, we were Cycle 9. They'd had eight other audiences to hone these performances with and really find the best way to sell it. It felt repetitive to the point of tedium to me, but they never wavered.

"America's Next Top Model is sitting inside this room," they said. "Really think about that. Look around. This is your competition. You are the select few. Does anyone know how many girls tried out for this show?"

We all shook our heads. They all smiled.

"A lot. Thousands upon thousands. Ten thousand tried out in Boston alone."

I looked at the few other girls whom I recognized from the Boston tryouts with wide eyes.

"And it wasn't just the auditions. Thousands upon thousands sent in audition tapes from all over the country. Every single state. We had casting scouts all over looking for candidates. And you guys are the ones who made it. You're here. And it's not just your looks. You all know that being a top model is more than that. It's who you are. And one of you . . . is America's Next Top Model. This is a once-in-a-lifetime opportunity."

They kept going. And going. I was uncomfortable with this level of flattery. In *Cultish: The Language of Fanaticism*, Amanda Montell describes this tactic used by cult leaders: "When you convince someone that they're above everyone else, it helps you both distance them from outsiders and also abuse them, because you can paint anything from physical assault to unpaid labor to verbal attacks as 'special treatment' reserved only for them."

On the one hand, I desperately wanted to feel special. I was one of the select few! On the other hand, this whole process had felt so random, it had never once felt like I was actually doing anything particularly special.

"This experience can only be what you make of it," they said, for the first time of many.

Suddenly their tones and demeanor shifted. They had been serious and kind, and now there was something else in the air. One of them stepped out from the line they'd been in.

"That information is worth more than you know. If you do anything to put that information at risk, we will sue you for five million dollars." He paused for effect. The NDA section of the contract carried, famously, a fine of five million dollars if violated, as Janice Dickinson once bemoaned in a red-carpet interview.

A gorgeous, long-limbed bartender from Boston with a lazy eye and an accent so thick I wanted to cut into it like it was a rib eye broke the silence. "Yeah, but, like . . . I don't have five million dollahs."

"We know you don't. We know all about all of your financial information. None of you have five million dollars. None of your families have five million dollars either."

We looked around at one another as we all realized that, yes, of course, that was true. We'd given them detailed accounts of our personal financial information as well as our families' before we'd even received our plane tickets.

"What you need to understand is we won't just sue you. We'll sue your entire family. And I don't just mean your parents. We'll sue your kids . . ."

Boston opened her mouth to say something, presumably that she didn't have any kids, that none of us did.

". . . by which I mean your future kids. We'll sue your children, we'll sue your children's children, we'll sue your children's children's children."

I swallowed the lump in my throat. *How would that even work?* I wondered.

"Sorry, but . . . how would that even work?" a girl asked, and I was so relieved.

"Great question," said the producer sincerely. "Here's how it would work: we would sue you and win. And the judge will decide how much we get to dock your pay for the rest of your life. For the rest of your life, every dollar you earn, we will get a cut. We will garnish your wages for the rest of your life. And after you die, we'll get a percentage of every dollar your children earn, and their children, and on and on, until we get five million dollars plus interest. If you say anything to anyone, you will be paying us back long after you are dead. You will never achieve any level of success without us taking a huge chunk of it. Buying a house, putting your kids through college, finishing college yourself—all of that will be impossible."

Kids and a house felt impossibly out of reach already. And the meeting just kept going: hours of them hammering the same point over and over. I desperately wanted them to know that I would be one of the "good ones" who would do what she was told and wouldn't cause them any trouble. But I knew that there was no way to make them see that. There was no way to make them see me at all. They weren't performing for us; they were performing for the contract and for the money that it guaranteed them. They were performing for the promise of good TV. And unlike my hypothetical kids and house, it wasn't out of reach. They knew what they wanted and exactly how to get it.

"There's a million girls that would happily take your place," they kept saying. "And we have their phone numbers. They're ready and willing to meet us on the next island."

That night at dinner, I sat pushing the food around on my plate, still stunned into silence. As a kid, I was painfully shy. Every report card I brought home from elementary school said that I was smart and capable but never spoke up in class. I had one friend, which I thought was more than enough. After years of badgering me to invite people to my birthday parties, my mom finally asked me what I really wanted to do. I told her I wanted to spend the night at a hotel. So she got us a room at the local Motel 6 for the night. I swam in the pool for hours; we ate cake in bed and watched all the late-night talk shows. I loved seeing the comedians do stand-up. It was my favorite birthday ever.

In fifth grade, I discovered that I could do more than just watch comedy on late-night shows: I could use it to overcome my crippling social anxiety. I slowly came out of my shell. Making people laugh was the only way I really knew how to connect with people, but after the lecture that day, I didn't feel very funny. So I reverted to my childhood self: Shy. Silent.

That's why Ebony and I were perfect cruise ship roommates: we were both introverts who could fake it when we had to. When I met Ebony, my first thought was: *She's going to win.* In a group of the most beautiful girls I'd ever seen, she stood out head and shoulders above the rest. Literally: she was over six feet tall and wore her hair in a big, messy bun on top of her head that made her even taller. When we first got to our room, she seemed shy, sweet, guarded, and deeply insecure. Then we went to dinner, and I watched her become a different person for the camera.

"I didn't come here to make friends," she said in the van. "I'll start remembering y'all's names when we make it to the house."

But in our room, she was different.

"I want to be smart about this. I'm trying to be, like, the bitch or whatever, but it's harder than I thought," she told me.

Oftentimes, we wouldn't talk much in the room: we both needed quiet and space (at least as much quiet and space as possible in a forty-eight-square-foot room). That night, we said even less than usual.

"That was . . . pretty crazy," I said.

"Dinner?" she asked.

"No, the talk about the contract," I answered.

"Shit, yeah! That *was* crazy! I didn't know how to act at dinner after all that."

"Oh my god, me too!" I said, relieved again. "I didn't even know how to be a normal person!"

We agreed that it was wild and way too long and we were glad it was over. None of us were going to be forgetting any of that anytime soon—surely that was the end of it.

The Very Scary Producers and Lawyers gave us the Talk AGAIN in which we were threatened with defamation, disembowelment, and death if we breathed a peep of anything to anyone. They are, let me say, not at all fucking around, and I FUCKING GET IT, I wrote in my journal several long, repetitive days later.

Over and over, we heard that "America's Next Top Model is in this room," "this is a once-in-a-lifetime opportunity," "this experience is only what you make of it," and "we will garnish your wages for the rest of your life." These phrases started rattling around in my mind, like a song that gets stuck in your head.

Of course, it wasn't just our contracts that we were dealing with; there was also the deal between the cruise line and the network, and, on that front, there was some tension. Specifically, between the show and the passengers, who hated us. One day, we were divided into three groups and led to a part of the ship we'd never been to before. One group was taken to the climbing wall, one to the skating rink, and my group was brought to the hot tub. A production assistant arranged us around the hot tub, some girls sitting with just their feet in the water, and a few of us, including me, sitting in the water. I was in the middle, submerged almost to my neck.

"I hope we can go in the pool after this," I said, slowly cooking in the water.

"No talking yet," said one of the cameramen.

"Sorry," I said. "Oh, and sorry for saying sorry. Fuck."

Eventually, they got the angles and lighting right and called action, and we were allowed to talk. Allowed to talk and contractually obligated to look like we were having the time of our lives.

"I hope I can go in the pool after this," I said.

"Smile," said the cameraman.

"Sorry," I said.

We all turned bright red, and they had to pump us full of water and juice to keep our energy up. As they were wrapping up the shoot, I asked one of the crew members if we could go in the pool to cool off.

"Sorry," he answered, "we've already been here too long; they have to open it back up for the passengers."

I looked over at the entrance to the pool area, and there was an angry horde gearing up. The crew hurried us back inside to avoid another confrontation. A few crew members had to help one of the girls walk inside; she'd gotten so overheated she was wobbling on her feet like a baby deer. They covered our heads with towels to make sure no one could take a picture.

We still never knew where we were going at any given time or, indeed, what time it was. We barely knew one another—we just got little glimpses. A girl who didn't make it past the first elimination would sneak glances at crew members' or passengers' watches, and she'd tell us what time it was a few times a day. "It's ten thirty, pass it on," she'd whisper.

"A.m. or p.m.?" we'd joke, because we were so disoriented sometimes, we could barely tell.

The days blurred together. Soon after reboarding the ship at Saint John's, when we were whittled down from thirty-three to twenty, we had to sit through the Talk again, this time with network executives and lawyers, who reminded us we were one step closer, but first they had to do some interviews.

Throughout that process, we learned that the word "producer" covers a lot of ground on a TV set. We were interviewed by executive producers, supervising producers, senior producers, associate producers. We also learned that the word "crew" referred to anyone who worked for the production company that made the show, from the sound guys and PAs to the executive producers. Even the psychologists were crew members. We each had another brief session with a different psychologist, Dr. Suzanne

Zachary, a blond woman with a round face and glasses who asked me if I had any questions.

"A million," I said, "but I can't think of any."

"That's fair," she said, before sending me on my way.

And then, when we were just about ready to explode from talking and hearing and thinking about ourselves, they told us that everyone we'd been talking to so far worked for the show's production company, and now it was time to talk to the producers from the network that would air the show.

We were all sprawled around the room in our usual spots, waiting to be lectured or interviewed again, when a man we hadn't seen before walked in. We all straightened up a little and put our game faces on, preparing ourselves to be lectured again. He ignored all of us and walked through the room, carefully stepping around all our legs and hands, to a TV. He muttered and swore at it for a little while before turning on the screen. Another man's face was on it. We stared at it, wondering if we'd reached the audiovisual section of the performance.

"Hi, girls!" he said, and we all jumped. He could see us! He was in a conference room of his own, all the way in Los Angeles.

How is his face on this TV in the middle of the damn ocean?! I wondered.

He was staring at us, looking us all up and down. "It's so nice to see all of your faces, I've heard so much about you," he said.

I was tired and cranky and, through no fault of his, hated him. The sound of his voice made me shiver.

"America's Next Top Model is in this room, you know."

I tried not to visibly wince.

He had us go around and say our names and where we were from, then sent us out, and the production company producers walked in, presumably to share all their notes with him. They had us sit and wait, giving us our books and journals until they were ready to take us to our next destination.

By the end of it, I was sick of myself. But at the same time, I had no idea who I was or, more important, who the producers wanted me to be.

That night, at dinner, Tyra came in and had us all stand up and tell her why we deserved to make it off the cruise ship and into the house. I have no idea what I said. Nothing very articulate—it didn't make it to air. The other plus-size contestant, Tara, gave a beautiful, fiery, impassioned speech about how, actually, America deserved a plus-size top model. *Crap,* I thought as she sat down. *I wish I had said . . . any of that.* Her speech didn't make it to air either.

Part of why it was so hard to think was all the seasickness. Girls had been sick on and off the whole trip. Victoria Marshman got so ill the first night that it made it to air, but we were all slightly nauseated most of the time. Sitting for hours in windowless rooms in the middle of the rocking open sea is not exactly conducive to a happy inner ear. The crew had been handing out motion sickness bracelets and Dramamine as needed. But tonight, the ship was rocking more violently than ever, and even in the dining room with its big windows, we were all pretty green. I was terrified that either I or someone near me was going to throw up.

We were all running on little to no sleep and little to no food, lurching around on a boat, dying to hear if the last week of work and waiting was going to pay off. Emotions were high. After dinner, the crew set up for the elimination that would determine which of us would make it into the house. It was clearly a large-scale production: there were more crew members than I'd ever seen in one place. The other contestants and I all sat silently, watching them put together a stage where, presumably, our fates would be revealed.

After an hour or so, they led us out to the elaborate runway and stage they'd built over one of the pools. It was made out of clear Plexiglas and lit from underneath by purple lights. *That looks like something out of a CW show,* I thought before realizing . . . it was. I can still remember the shaky little tippity taps of forty heels walking up the stairs and clickety clacking over the platform. It gave me vertigo. Or was it nerves? Or was it the ship? We held on to one another for support, both emotional and physical.

Like she would so many times to come, Tyra stood at the end of the stage. The energy was electric. We were all poised and ready to go. Suddenly a man was screaming. We all looked around. I thought maybe a passenger had finally snapped and was telling us off.

Ken Mok, the creator of the show and its executive producer, was standing off to the side, screaming at a cruise ship employee while a sound guy stood next to him, wishing he were anywhere else.

"Tell them if they don't turn the fucking music off, I will rip those speakers out myself!" Ken yelled, spitting and red in the face.

We were all on a razor-thin edge. At the absolute height of emotions with nowhere for them to go, as we were still unable to talk. I stared at Tyra. She was so beautiful and had all the trappings of celebrity. Her clothes, hair, and makeup—everything was picture-perfect. A TV character come to life in front of my eyes. *But she's real,* I reminded myself. *She's a real woman, flesh and blood.* I ached for access to her in a way that wasn't realistic or possible, and I knew it. I just wanted to climb over the bridge between us, but to her, I was a face in the crowd. One of many, nine times over. But to me, she was everything. She held my future in her hands.

And I knew that I would never be as important to her as she was to me, but I closed my eyes and prayed that she would give us all a sign that everything was okay, that we would be okay, no matter what happened.

"Can we do something about this slippery stage?" she said. "We're all on here looking like we're on a Slip 'N Slide or something." She winked at us conspiratorially. I smiled ear to ear back at her.

A PA came around and put duct tape squares on the bottoms of all our heels, and the director called action.

"Here we are, ladies," Tyra said. "The top twenty baddest chicks in the bunch. But of course, there can only be thirteen. Thirteen girls who will become Cinderella stories. They'll go from everyday girls in their hometowns to girls that everyone in America will know their name."

She started calling names:

"Mila," she said, and Mila Bouzinova strode forward confidently, flipped her hair over her shoulder, and hugged Tyra. Tyra looked at someone off camera and shook her head.

"No more hugs," they yelled.

She kept reading names. Some girls were already crying when she started, and with each name, they wept harder. When she called my name, I started like a horse and yelled, "Nuh-uh!" As I carefully walked across the platform toward Tyra, I looked in her eyes and thought, *God, I can't wait to go to sleep.*

"Watch your step," she said as I slid a little.

As each name got called, the reactions got bigger and bigger.

"You scared me, girl!" cried Ebony, jubilant.

"Words cannot describe, oh my god," said Heather Kuzmich, her face in her hands.

Lisa was the last to be called, and she could barely make it over the platform, shaking and crying, into Tyra's open arms. "This is the happiest day of my life," she said.

"You thirteen are over there because being America's Next

Top Model is not just about being pretty and taking pretty pictures," said Tyra, "but about being role models. And that's why you're standing over there today. Congratulations!"

We all screamed and jumped up and down.

"No more tears!" said Victoria to me as we hugged. "Why are you crying?"

"I have no idea!" I said, and meant it.

We said our goodbyes to the girls who didn't make it. Tara didn't make it. I didn't understand why, but I was also relieved I wouldn't have to compete against her. That night I thought, *This is it. Now we fly home and pack up for the adventure of a lifetime.*

"You have one more meeting left," the handler told us, and I wanted to cry. I wanted to tell them I would do whatever they wanted if they would just leave me alone.

Their tone at this final meeting was even more dire than usual.

"America's Next Top Model is in this room. You did it."

"Think of all those girls out there who cried themselves to sleep. You owe it to them not to mess this up."

"We chose you for a reason. Don't make us regret it. Because we will make you regret it. Believe that."

I did.

For the last time, we sat on the floor of the ship, just letting what were now old, familiar adages wash over us. They had brought us in right after breakfast the morning after the elimination, around nine a.m. By the time we left that room, it was afternoon. In writing this, I was sure that my brain had exaggerated the memory, so I checked with a few other contestants.

"Was it really hours?" I asked Brittany Hatch, a straight-shooting, down-to-earth woman who was on Cycle 6.

"It was hours," she said.

"Was it really hours?" I texted Jenah Doucette, who was on my cycle.

"BRUH," she responded. "They literally used, like, scare tactics. I thought I was going to get sued and have my wages garnished for the rest of my life."

I was struck by her phrasing—the exact same words that I still remember and still use after all these years. Suddenly, the constant repetition made sense: they were drilling it into our heads not just so we would remember it, but so that the jargon would create a world that we would buy into, body and soul. They were trying to cram what many cults do over weeks and months into just a few days. In *Cultish*, Amanda Montell describes this phenomenon: "When repeated over and over again, speech has meaningful, consequential power to construct and constrain our reality . . . Without us even noticing, our very understanding of ourselves and what we believe to be true becomes bound up with the group. With the leader. All because of language." We were bound up, all right.

The contract was the glue that held everything together. We'd signed it; we'd had it explained to us for hours and hours. We were in this thing. There was no going back now; we were already in too deep.

But how much legal water did it hold? "You can't sign away your rights for future harm," pointed out Sarah Rhoades, from Cycle 5, as we compared notes. Maybe in a court of law we can't. But standing on that Plexiglas platform, shaking and crying in our heels, we did without a second thought.

AFTER THE CRUISE SHIP, we were sent home for two weeks before they flew us out to Los Angeles and the house. Those two weeks felt like the languid days between Christmas and New Year's. There are things to do, but time doesn't make sense. I had a packing list they'd given me with everything we'd need to be away from home for months. One of the items was childhood photos, for the montage they showed for the winner. I sat with my mom going through all our photo albums, imagining the pictures splayed across TVs all across the country.

"Look at this one!" she'd say, tearing up. "You were the most beautiful baby."

Another item on the list was "as many cigarettes as you can smoke in two months." I did a little math and realized that I would need a carton, which I absolutely could not afford. I couldn't bring myself to ask my mom for money. She was newly divorced and desperately trying to be a cool mom, but I didn't think she was ready to be *that* cool. So I scrounged in her couch, her car, every nook and cranny of my bedroom, and finally came up with enough coins to drop on the counter at the only gas station in town.

I sat in the Cambridge Farms parking lot, staring down at my first and only carton of cigarettes. *I am going to smoke these in a Hollywood mansion,* I thought. But that was then. For now, I was sitting in a gas station parking lot trying to shake off the humiliation of paying for a carton of Camel Light cigarettes with fistfuls of dirty coins.

5

I'm a Fucking
Ringtone

et's go back in time, all the way to the early aughts. Trump is
just an annoying pseudo-businessman who crops up in the
occasional television appearance, the housing bubble is still being
inflated, and, most important, ringtones are a multibillion-dollar
industry. You've even picked out the very ringtone you want to
buy on Jamster to put on your pink bedazzled Motorola Razr.

I, Sarah Hartshorne, was a ringtone. For $1.29 you could hear
my tinny little voice coming out of your flip phone. I don't know
if anyone ever did, but the point is: they could have. The CW
marketing team responsible could never have predicted that between the time we recorded the ringtones on a soundstage in Los
Angeles and the time the show came out, ringtone downloads
would plummet in popularity. Still, I was a fucking ringtone.

To get to that recording session, I had to go from the middle
of a Plexiglas runway atop the deep end of a pool on the deck of
a cruise ship in the Caribbean Sea to a brief stint back in Boston
to, finally, Los Angeles. Almost immediately after we landed at
LAX, we surrendered our phones, our iPods, all our IDs, and
our cash and credit cards to an associate producer. We also confirmed that we'd deleted all our social media accounts and had

any pictures of us online taken down. Then we were taken to a hotel that felt like a horror movie set: every painting was slightly crooked, and there were mysterious stains all over the concrete stairs that wrapped around the building. "It was so creepy," Kimberly agreed, but in reality, "it was just some random Holiday Inn," she recalled when I interviewed her for this book. And after we were settled, we were brought to yet another conference room, complete with burn marks in the carpet. I looked around at the women in the room—my competition. The cruise ship felt like a distant dream, and I could barely remember any of their names, except for Ebony, who smiled and waved at me. I waved back and gave her a look to say, *How weird is this?* She nodded and shrugged.

Then in walked Michelle Mock-Falcon, the casting director who'd taken us for smoke breaks on the cruise ship. I wondered if we were going to have to hear the same old speech yet again, but she had something new to tell us. She broke down all the things we needed to know before we started and a few tips.

"She was, like, debriefing us, giving us the rules. Like, 'You guys can't talk when the cameras aren't on, but you're going to want to talk as much as you can when the cameras are on so you're relevant,'" Kimberly remembered.

"This opportunity is what you make of it," Michelle told us, echoing what we'd heard on the ship. "Make your presence known."

It was good advice that I never managed to follow. I had no strategy for making my presence known. Not knowing what day or time it was rendered my critical thinking skills useless. I could only face what was in front of me. My only plan was to copy whatever the other girls did. As soon as we were allowed to talk to one another, that is.

Michelle also explained why weren't allowed to talk so often.

"Sometimes," she told us, "the producers will put you on ice. When that happens, it is in all of your best interest to listen, or they will make your life really difficult."

"On ice," she explained, means the time when reality show contestants are off camera and, therefore, are not allowed to talk. The producers, she told us, wanted to capture every interaction between the contestants, so if we weren't being filmed, we had to be silent, lest the cameras miss something. This had the added benefit of silencing contestants into submission and making us feel isolated and crazy. Montell says this is typical of "oppressive cultish environments . . . No communication, no solidarity. No chance to figure a way out."

Not that any of us wanted out (yet). We all still desperately wanted to be there. To be at the house. To get started on this adventure for real. But around every corner was yet another windowless conference room. And just when it felt like maybe this whole thing was an elaborate practical joke meets purgatory . . . we were brought to a set.

The set was on a real live Hollywood soundstage on a studio lot just like in *Singin' in the Rain,* which I'd watched hundreds of times as a kid. Finally, after all the terrifying lectures and interviews and blood tests, my Hollywood fantasy was coming to life. The set had giant metal tunnels and pipes mounted at various angles on the wall: very "early 2000s music video vibes," Kimberly recalled. Off to the side were racks of avant-garde, futuristic designer clothing made of metal and leather and Lucite. Two tiny, blasé-looking stylists in shapeless but chic black outfits clutched coffees the size of their heads and gazed upon rows and rows of terrifying-looking heels. *They look just like stylists should look,* I thought. Endless hair and makeup rooms were full of yawning, shuffling makeup artists setting up elaborate kits of more products than I knew even existed. *No wonder it's called a Production!* I wrote in my journal.

Outside, there was a food truck parked with the sun rising over Los Angeles behind it. Models sat perched on picnic tables in various stages of hair, makeup, and wakefulness, staring sleepily at their breakfast burritos and burying their perfect faces in their coffees. I could see other sets and crews in the distance. I sipped my coffee and (quietly—no talking!) lived out all my wide-eyed ingenue fantasies. I might have been wearing low-slung bootcut jeans and a tank top from Old Navy, but in my head, I was in a pert blue Kitty Foyle dress sewn by my ma back home before she'd put me on a bus bound for Hollywood stardom. It's probably a good thing we weren't allowed to talk. I would have been insufferable.

After a while, a crew member with a clipboard came and called my name. "Sarah?"

"Yes! Me!" I said, jumping up and out of my fantasy.

She gestured to follow her and walked me to a small room full of recording equipment.

"Take a seat," said the sound guy, gesturing to a stool with studio headphones and a microphone on it. He handed me promos for local CW stations. I realized we were here to make all the promotional materials for the show. They would have to do all this now before girls got eliminated and went home. This was the last time we'd all really be together. Anxiety filled my brain like a jet of dark squid ink in water.

I couldn't imagine going through all of this, packing up everything I owned and setting my life aside, only to immediately be sent home. I started to panic. I looked down at the scripts in my hand and forced my eyes to make out the shapes in front of me. A real script, with words just for me. Nothing to do but do it.

"Do you watch your local CW channel? Looks like it's . . . CW Springfield?" asked the engineer, a friendly, bearlike man.

"No," I said honestly. "I'm from a really small town. We don't get cable. Springfield is, like, an hour and a half away."

"Wait, there's no TV in your hometown? That is wild!"

"Yeah, but they're going to carpool in one horse and carriage to go watch it somewhere," I joked.

"You're funny—this is going to be great. Let's do a take. Give it a lot of personality."

"Oy, oy, it's Sarah from *Top Model* 'ere," I bellowed in an over-the-top Cockney accent. "Right 'ere on the ol' CW! Don't go anywheres!"

Laughter exploded throughout the room. It should have been mortifying, but it actually felt amazing. If I could make them laugh, I could avoid panicking.

"Not that kind of personality. Just be yourself."

"Yeah, okay, sorry!" I said.

"No, no, don't be sorry, honestly. You're doing great," said another crew member. "It's always easier to tone it down than try and crank it up. We're going to get some really good stuff today."

"Hi, this is Sarah Hartshorne from *America's Next Top Model*, right here on the CW22 in Springfield. Don't go away," I said, with all the enthusiasm in the world. I was pretty sure that this was the closest I was ever going to come to waving a CGI wand and inviting people to keep watching the Disney Channel. I was determined to make the most of it. We recorded a few more, and then it was time to do ringtones.

"I'm going to be a ringtone?!" I said.

"You sure are," came the answer from the soundboard. I grinned.

"Hey, hey," I crooned. "Sarah from *Top Model* here. Pick up the phone!"

"Stop smizing! Your phone is ringing!"

"You wanna be on top? Then answer the phone!"

After I was done, the engineer popped his head out and told me something that would carry me through the next week.

"You're funny. You'll do well. You and Kimberly, you guys should have a TV show together."

The handler came back and walked me, smile plastered on my face, across the soundstage, which was loud and jarring after the tiny, soundproofed booth, to the hair and makeup room, which immediately felt like a respite from all the craziness outside. No one in here was holding a clipboard, and the energy was relaxed and friendly. I was escorted to a chair, and as I sat, my shoulders relaxed a little.

"You have gorgeous skin," said the makeup artist, and I blushed to my bones.

"Thank you," I whispered.

"Why are you whispering?" she asked.

"Are . . . are we allowed to talk to you?"

"Oh," she answered, "I don't know, probably not. Whatever, it's fine. Ken's not here."

"He better not be! I have no time for that man's shit," said another makeup artist, and they all laughed.

I was scandalized and delighted. I felt like I'd been allowed to hang with the cool girls who smoked behind my high school. They were so nonchalant about the rules that had been hammered (and hammered and hammered and hammered) into us.

The hairstylist pulled my hair into a bun so tight my face looked like Norma Desmond's and I was ready for my close-up. This was my first real photo shoot, although I told myself it didn't *really* count because they hadn't started filming yet. We were shooting the promotional materials for the show, so these pictures wouldn't be judged by anyone except audiences at home.

The dress I'd been assigned for the shoot was made of chain mail. I had to hold on to the Lilliputian stylists to carefully step into it, and I was terrified of toppling over and bringing them down with me. Then they jacked me up onto giant, pointe-toed heels that I couldn't even stand in, let alone walk. Two PAs led me to set, slowly and carefully, like a chic spirit walker. They had me posing near a bunch of pipes so I could hold on to them to prop myself up on. Very Tank Girl meets *Teen Vogue*.

After some lighting tests, the shoot got underway. I kept feeling the anxiety trying to creep back in, but there was too much to think about. It felt good to have my brain be fully occupied and to be able to focus on my body. What was my face doing? Where was my light? I kept my head up and just tried my damnedest to look like I'd had my photograph professionally taken lots of times, and not just at the JCPenney in Holyoke, Massachusetts, wearing a matching outfit with my mom.

Somehow, it was going well. I couldn't believe it. The photographer kept saying what I'd always imagined a photographer *should* say: "Yes, just like that. Chin down. Fierce, girl, yes." If this was the hard part of the show, I was feeling pretty damn confident. This was fun as hell.

"Oh my god, did I smize?" I asked.

"You totally smized," said the photographer.

My support team came and led me away to a room full of the other girls and helped me take off my shoes. Once they were gone, I could take in the rest of the contestants. We were all decked out in futuristic gear: I had my chain mail dress, and Kimberly had on a clear plastic peplum corset top. Jenah and Heather both had on shiny black pleather and black lipstick. Our hair was all slick and equally shiny. We sat around awkwardly, unable to talk about how ridiculous we all looked and felt. Slowly but surely, a fit of giggles crawled up from my stomach, into my throat, and up to my face, until I was absolutely weeping and wheezing with laughter. The laughs cut through the air and ricocheted off the drop ceiling like a cannonball. A few girls looked at me like I was crazy, and a few joined in. It's hard to shake with laughter in a dress made out of metal, or Lucite, or latex, but we managed. The PAs assigned to watch us just rolled their eyes. At least we weren't talking.

After a while, we were led back out to the main room, where the set had been redone to hold all of us for a group photo. The photographer's assistants set to work getting us in position. There was a piece of tape on the floor in the middle of all of us that marked where I assumed Tyra would be photoshopped in later. The air was loaded. The crew was tired—it had been a long day— but I was still running on adrenaline. It was hard to know because we couldn't talk, but as I looked around to size everyone up, it felt like I was getting sized up right back. Of course, I was also looking at everyone's physical size and comparing it with mine. I wondered if they could all instantly tell that I was the plus-size contestant.

As we were paraded out to set and put into our positions, I looked around at their thin frames and sky-high legs and thought, *Oh no. This is what real models look like.* I was embarrassed by my earlier confidence on set. A switch had been flipped; what had been glamorous and exciting was now ugly and fat and terrifying. All day I'd been shaking it off, clearing my brain of all those inky jets of anxiety, but I couldn't shake this.

When it was time for a break, my two support PAs came over and led me to a seat. It took a minute for me to get situated and keep the dress safe, and between the three of us, we carefully set me on a chair. And then I had a terrible realization.

"I'm so sorry, I . . . I . . . I have to pee," I stammered.

They diligently walked back, gave me their arms, got me up,

and escorted me to a bathroom. "Can you make it there alone?" one asked.

I hauled myself through the door and held on to the walls. "Uh . . . no," I said. "I can't quite . . . reach."

A PA named Katie had to come and help me. A lot of the crew is a nameless, shapeless blur in my memory, but she is seared in there. Not least because she had to hold my arms and lower me onto a toilet like a child while I stared into her face and memorized it. Midstream, I had a thought.

I'm a fucking ringtone.

6

That Girl

After shooting the promo materials, we were driven to a bland building full of mirrored windows and empty escalators where we were to wait, yet again, in a windowless room and put on ice. A bored PA was in charge of making sure we didn't move or talk until a sound guy came to put our mic packs on. A murmur ran through the girls. I waited for it to reach me. "It's Mr. Jay," someone whispered at a barely audible volume. I whipped my head around. I didn't see him, but there was a charge in the air.

"Hold here for a few minutes, guys," they told us.

We sat with bated breath. This was it. It was time!

An hour later, someone had to shake me awake. Okay, *now* it was time. I sat up, bleary-eyed. Had the sound guys heard me snoring? I gamely trotted after everyone, a little unsteady on my feet. We walked into the building, and there was Mr. Jay!

"Oh, shit!" said Bianca Golden. "It's happening!"

"Cut!" called the director of photography, before we could even react. Mr. Jay immediately looked down at his phone, which was unlike anything I'd ever seen before: the first ever iPhone. "Now when we start filming again," the director said, "you have to cheer and scream like Mr. Jay is the most exciting thing you've ever seen."

No problem. He *was* one of the most exciting things I'd ever seen.

When they called action, we all went to scream.

"Hello!" interrupted Mr. Jay.

There was a slight pause. The woos were still halfway out of our mouths. We looked around, unsure of what to do with the unfinished excitement.

"Cut! We have to do that again. Do you want to say hello, or can they just cheer when they see you?" said the director of photography.

"Either way," said Mr. Jay politely, although he looked like he would rather be getting a root canal.

"Okay, this time Mr. Jay is going to say hello, and then remember, you guys, scream like it's the most exciting thing you've ever seen."

We stood, a little less assured, waiting. There was a long pause. Mr. Jay looked like he was bracing himself for impact. He looked down, rubbed his temples, and slowly looked up, his face a perfectly contoured and coiffed mask with an eerie, plastic smile that made him look like he'd been photoshopped into this world.

We waited.

"Hello!" he said.

We screamed.

"We are in downtown Los Angeles, in the Fashion District, which is the center of California's fashion industry. And now, I've got something special to show you, so come with me," he continued.

"Cut!" yelled the director.

The same bored PA brought us back to holding.

"Can I go to the bathroom?" asked one of the girls.

"No," replied the PA. It never got less surprising to hear that. The girl sat down.

A few minutes later Victoria asked, "Can I go to the bathroom?"

"No."

"Why?"

"We don't have time to take you; we're going to start soon."

We sat and waited for an uncomfortably long time—more than enough time to have gone and come back. We all stared, boring holes into her head with our eyes.

"Look, I'm sorry, but we really can't take you right now. We don't have anyone to go with you, it's all hands on deck to get the shot set up, and the director is freaking out because we lost the light."

Well, at least I knew it was dark out now—which, I realized, meant we'd been at this for about seventeen hours. It felt like someone was sitting on my eyelids. I couldn't even imagine how tired the crew must be. When I interviewed production staff for this book, they often felt the same way about us. "If it's awful for me as a production staff member, it was definitely way worse for the contestants, because you guys were just sitting around for so many hours, you weren't allowed to talk to each other," said one.

"We got breaks, and a break is when you can control your time," said another. "You guys couldn't even go to the bathroom when you wanted."

Eventually, they brought us out to a dark parking lot. *Ah,* I thought, *the jig is up. Finally, we're going to be murdered.* Instead, the crew parted and revealed Mr. Jay, standing in front of a flowery green passenger van with "Green Is the New Black: 100% Biodiesel" scrawled across the top. The theme of our cycle was, apparently, the environment. As one of the contestants, Mila, said, "It's important to be aware of what keeps our earth good and stuff." That about summed up the show's actual commitment to being eco-conscious.

Mr. Jay stood there, his hair pristine, his face perfectly made up and miserable.

"Girls," he said, "this is going to be your vehicle for the entire competition. Now, it's time for this green machine to take you to your house, and then tomorrow, you're gonna have your first photo shoot."

We screamed and loaded into the van. It was beautiful and very on theme. The windows were covered with a decorative skin that made it look like we were driving through the rain forest. There was fake grass and faux wood paneling surrounding the pleather seats (made of recycled tires!). There was a giant picture of Tyra mounted on the back wall of the van (with a green leaf in front of her face!). There was a minifridge stocked with tiny plastic water bottles (*womp womp*).

We all jumped up and down, dancing and yelling, "We're going to the house! We're going to the house!" There were two crew members in the back with us, one camera guy and one sound guy. We quieted down pretty quickly once the reality of driving around with blacked-out windows became clear. Everyone started to look a little gray.

Within minutes, Lisa said, "Guys, I'm so sorry. I get really carsick." After a few more minutes she turned to one of the crew guys and said quietly, "Can we pull over?"

He looked like a deer caught in headlights, saying nothing and looking around as if for an escape route. He opened and closed his mouth. He looked at us. We looked at him.

"Pull over!" we finally yelled.

He mumbled into his walkie-talkie, and we heard back, "Negative, tell them they just have to deal." He looked at us. We looked back at him.

"I really don't feel so good," said Lisa. We looked at her, looked at him, and then all chimed in at once, talking over one another in an angry, queasy cacophony.

"Seriously, pull over!"

"Pull the fuck over!"

"What is the matter with you?!"

He just looked back with big, confused eyes. I almost felt bad for him. Almost.

After what felt like a very winding and hilly forever, the van stopped, and I realized that I'd been tensing every muscle in my body the entire ride. We continued to wait while the crew got set up to film us getting out of the van and going into the house. I rocked back and forth in sheer anticipation. The house had become this beacon of shining light, the promised land I was starting to feel like I would never reach. And now it was within sight. Or would have been, if the windows weren't blacked out.

When they let us in the house, we took off like banshees, running and screaming with excitement about every nook and cranny. The entryway closet had been reimagined into a tiny little den, with a camera mounted on one wall facing a big, comfy armchair. It felt like something out of *Seventeen* magazine, with the plush pink rug and fake plants and Astroturf on the wall.

"This must be the confessional!" said one of the other girls. We all screamed in excitement. The confessional! From what I'd gleaned from watching the show, this was where all the juicy moments happened. The tiny little room with no crew members in it where we were to spill our deepest, darkest secrets.

Next to that was the kitchen, which was all stainless steel and sleek marble countertops; everything was silver and white. It was very of the time, straight out of 2007 HGTV. "Oh my god, look at this *kitchen!*" someone yelled.

In the back of the kitchen was a door leading to a beautiful patio with couches and lounge chairs and stairs leading down to a pool and a hot tub. Now it was my turn to scream: "Oh my god, look at the pool!" If you learn one thing about me, let it be this: I love a pool, and I *love* a hot tub. For me, the exploration ended there. I'd found my favorite part of the house, where I would be spending every spare minute. Incidentally, if you compiled all the group shots of us reading Tyra Mail, you would see I'm in my swimsuit and a towel almost every single time.

I went to strip down to my underwear and dive right in when I realized with a pang that doing so would probably guarantee me airtime, which, I knew, should have been added incentive, but instead it made me self-conscious. I thought back to Michelle's advice: *Make your presence known.* I headed back inside to join the other girls.

Not very reality TV star of you, I scolded myself.

"Okay," said Jenah, "seriously, who wants to go skinny-dipping?"

"Oh my god," I said, so relieved. "I do! Let's go!"

We all stripped out of our clothes and mic packs.

"I am going to be the first one in!" cried Lisa.

I shrieked with competitive laughter and started tearing off my clothes even faster. I'd be damned if she beat me in.

Once I was in the pool, my body relaxed a little. In a place where everything felt foreign, the familiar sensation of the water around my body was a balm. I took a deep breath and looked around. Lisa was doing the same thing.

"I've never even been near a house this fancy," she said.

I was surprised. All I knew about her so far was that she dressed well and was from Connecticut, so I had assumed she grew up rich. "Oh," I said. "I thought . . . I thought maybe you came from a house like this. Doesn't everyone in Connecticut have a pool?"

"Girl, no," she said. "I grew up in foster care."

"Oh," I said, embarrassed that I'd gotten her so wrong. "I'm sorry."

"It's okay," she said. "I'm out now. I'm here."

She was so matter-of-fact, so unafraid to talk about her pain and trauma. It brought up a jealousy within me that I didn't like. I resolved not to assume anything about any of the girls in the house. I wondered what they assumed about me.

We all went back inside and started to dry off and change in the bathroom. It was long and narrow, sort of railroad style. The sink was on one side, and on the other was a big spa bathtub with jets that I looked at wistfully. It was my dream bathtub, but I knew I'd never be brave enough to take a bath in front of all the girls, let alone the camera crew and the viewing audience at home. Luckily, the shower was a little more modest. I'd never seen anything like it, it was so luxurious. It was a walk-in with a clear glass door, but the rest of the walls were stone, up to about chest level on the average person, with glass above it reaching to the ceiling. Of course, we were all taller than the average person, so I was pretty sure our nipples would be, on occasion, above the modesty line. There were two showerheads, one an overhead rain showerhead, which I'd never seen before.

"There is one shower for all of you," one of the producers re-minded us. "Please keep that in mind when you are getting ready in the morning."

At least there were two toilets: two narrow individual stalls. I stepped inside one, wrapped in a towel, and took a brief moment to myself. These doors were the only ones in the whole house that we could close behind us. The rest were all sliding glass doors with no locks or the exterior doors, which we weren't allowed to touch.

The adrenaline was starting to wear off, and the almost twenty-hour-long day was starting to wear on me. I went outside, still wrapped in a towel, and lit a cigarette. I stared at all of Los Angeles spread out in front of me, sparkling and twinkling in the darkness. I knew I was in the midst of my life changing. Everything felt loaded, ready to explode.

Chantal Jones walked out and joined me in quietly staring at the city lights. A tear ran down her cheek. She looked like a movie star.

"Are you okay?" asked Mila, who was walking by.

"I'm . . . I'm amazing. I could not be better," Chantal answered, overcome with emotion.

"Then why are you crying?" asked Mila.

"I'm just so happy," said Chantal.

Chantal and I smiled at each other, and we all walked inside.

The downstairs room that looked out onto the pool was full of nine identical, neatly made beds with purple bedspreads and lime green sheets. Then there was a smaller room off the bathroom with four beds. All the girls who hadn't gone in the pool had claimed their beds, and no one seemed to want to be in the little room, but I didn't mind.

"This is like camp, y'all," said Chantal as she picked her bed.

"It really is," agreed Kimberly, "but like a fancy TV version."

At some point, the producers, who also seemed exhausted and at their wits' end, sat us down and laid out all the rules of the house

- Every morning, before we did anything else, we were to get mic'd. It absolutely had to be the first thing we did—before coffee, before a shower, and certainly before speaking to anyone. We could take the mic pack off while we were actively showering or swimming, but we had to put it back on *immediately* afterward.

- If we woke up in the middle of the night and wanted to walk around, we didn't have to get mic'd, but if anyone else woke up, we did, even if we didn't talk to each other. If there were two of us awake, we had to be mic'd.

- We were never to look directly into the camera (except for in the confessional) or talk to the camera operators. We shouldn't acknowledge them at all, even if they came rushing up to us, which they would do. A lot.

- We had to spend five minutes a day in the confessional. We didn't have to say anything, and we could go in with other people, but we all had to have been in the room for five minutes every day before any of us would be allowed to go to bed.

- In addition to the confessional, we would be interviewed by producers every day in a separate room dedicated for that purpose. During these interviews we should always be wearing the same outfit. We were to pick out our "interview outfit," and once we'd picked it, we couldn't change anything, not even jewelry or accessories. We were to bring our interview outfit with us wherever we went, just in case we had to change into it.

- They would not turn the lights off until everyone was in bed. If we were told to go to bed, we had to immediately, or there would be consequences. They didn't say what the consequences would be, but they didn't really have to. Their tone was ominous enough.

- Speaking of leaving the house, we were never to do so unless instructed and accompanied by the crew. All doors would remain locked, and if we were caught trying to get out, we would be punished. Not that we could have gotten far anyway: they'd taken our IDs, our credit cards and money, and our phones.

- There was absolutely no talking when the cameras were not on us. If someone told us we were on ice, all conversations had to cease completely. Failure by any of us to follow this rule would result in punishments for all of us.

- We would not be filmed in the toilet stalls if we were alone, but if there was more than one of us, we would be. The same went for the shower.

- We should consider showering together. You know, for the environment.

THAT NIGHT, as we were all lying in our identical twin beds, I realized this was the closest I'd ever come to sleepaway camp. As an only child who'd never shared a room or much of anything and loved nothing more than being alone, I was starting to wonder what the hell I'd gotten myself into. As I listened to the breathing of all the other girls in the room start to slow as they fell asleep, it started to sink in that every moment for the foreseeable future was going to be shared, not just with them but with the crew and, potentially, millions of viewers at home. What the fuck was I doing? And just when I was really panicking about how I would ever fall asleep, I was out like a light.

The next morning, we woke up after what felt like a solid fifteen minutes of sleep, and we all pitter-pattered into line to get mic'd by the sound guy. It was all foreign and exciting, our new morning routine.

"Morning," I said sleepily to Chantal.

"No talking," said a cameraman, who was filming the girls who were still in bed. He was one of a little gaggle of three people whom we would get very familiar with over the coming weeks, despite never being allowed to talk to them. There was one person holding a camera, one person holding a boom, and one person who was on the walkie-talkie, listening to instructions from a producer who was usually camped out in the wing of the house that was hidden from us. There were a few rooms downstairs that were accessible only via a door they'd disguised as a wall, and presumably that's where they were able to look at the footage from the security cameras that were mounted and hidden all over the house so they could tell the camera crews where to go. The camera crews were like roving packs of wild animals, on the hunt for drama.

When it was my turn, I walked up to the sound guy and put my arms up. The mic pack consisted of a little black rectangle that clipped to a big black strip of Velcro that he wrapped around our waists and a cord with a microphone, which snaked up and clipped to our shirt or our bra. We weren't really supposed to talk to the crew, in case it ruined a shot. But it felt wrong to have someone's arms around my waist without knowing his name. I took a chance and asked in a low voice, "What's your name?"

"Frank," he said.

"Hi, Frank. I'm Sarah."

"I know," he said.

"Right, right. Well, did you know that a blue whale's heart is the size of a golf cart?"

"I did not," he replied with a patient smile. "You got me there. You're all set."

I went upstairs to check out the kitchen, but of course, there was no food yet and, worse, no coffee. As I looked around, I realized that, as fancy as it seemed, there was no microwave or dishwasher. What kind of Hollywood Hills mansion doesn't have those basics? *How bizarre,* I thought.

WHEN PEOPLE ASK what filming was like, the adjective that swims to the top of the pile is "chaotic." We never knew what was coming or where we were going at any given time. We weren't allowed to have newspapers or magazines, except for preapproved fashion magazines that were covered in tape to hide the dates. Most of the time we weren't allowed to read our books (well-read girls don't make for good TV), and they'd taken our phones. It was hard to even find out what time it was, like at a casino. All the clocks on the appliances had been disabled, and the only time devices allowed were two tiny little alarm clocks that we all shared.

There was a phone for us to use, but it was turned on only during the preapproved phone times. The show had repurposed the space under the stairs as a cozy little phone nook. There was an upholstered bench and more fake plants (you know, for the environment).

One evening, almost a week in, at the end of a long day, a producer announced we had an hour and a half to make our first phone calls home, and we could divide that however we wanted. Saleisha Stowers and Janet, who acted as house mothers, sprang into action. One grabbed a notebook, and the other went to grab one of the alarm clocks to use as a timer.

"Okay, y'all," said Janet, doing some quick calculations, "that means we each get six and a half minutes. So, we need to keep it short. Get in, tell them you love them, you miss them, and get out."

"And be thinking about who you want to call while you're waiting," added Saleisha, who wrote her name down and handed off the notebook. "Write your names down here, and we'll go in that order. Let's go!"

"Not so fast," said the producer. "Before you get on the phone, remember: no details. Don't say anything that gives away what's been going on. You can say how you're feeling, but not why and not what happened. And no names. You can say 'the girls' or 'another girl,' but don't say who and don't say what they did."

I was buzzing with excitement. Normally, I'm not very sentimental when I travel away from loved ones. Even as a little kid, I had to be reminded to call home. But now, a familiar voice was exactly what I needed. We all filed in one by one. My name was toward the end of the list, so I paced around like a maniac. Finally, I settled down to wait next to Heather. We wrapped ourselves in blankets and sat on her bed, staring daggers at the booth.

Heather is on the autism spectrum, which the producers made a big deal about. She reminded me of almost everyone I went to high school with: quirky, artsy, passionate, and a little awkward at first. But she had a wicked sense of humor once you broke through that initial layer. She was constantly doodling, her long, dark hair falling in her face as she bent over the pages.

"Who are you going to talk to?" I asked Heather.

"My mom," she said.

"Aww," I said. "Are you guys close?"

"Yeah," she said. "I miss her. I miss everyone."

"Me too!" I said. "I can't wait to talk to my boyfriend."

"Aww, that's cute," she said.

"I know, gross, right?" I laughed. "I never thought I would be the girl who would miss her boyfriend."

"So gross. But who could have predicted any of"—she gestured to the mansion around us with her pale, graceful arm—"this?"

I laughed. It was true. I couldn't predict what was going to happen or how I was going to react. I felt like a stranger to myself. But maybe on the phone I could control the narrative, if only for six and a half minutes.

An hour and a half later, there were still three of us in line to talk on the phone, and the producer told us we were out of time.

"Are you crying?" Janet asked me, and I touched my cheek and felt tears, like the main character in a period drama. I was as surprised as anyone. I heard the frantic footsteps of the camera crew and I winced, knowing they were coming to film the very tears that had just caught me so off guard.

"I'm so sorry," I said, the tears pouring in earnest down my cheeks, mortified at the words coming out of my mouth. "I feel like such a drama queen. I just really wanted to talk to my boyfriend." *Who* was *I*?

And now here was the camera in my face, capturing it all. I sat down and put my face in my hands, which I knew was an even more dramatic thing to do, but I just wanted to hide.

"You crying because you can't call home and you're missing your man?" said Janet. I nodded. "Girl, this is hard, don't feel bad."

She was being so sweet. Everyone around me was being deferential to me, and it just made me cry harder in a vicious cycle. The producers waved the crew away so they wouldn't be on camera, and after some back-and-forth, they said that we could all get three extra minutes, but we shouldn't expect this kind of treatment going forward.

"This is a one-time thing, because it's your first time doing the phone thing," said David St. John, one of the supervising producers, who would go on to be an executive producer.

"Thank you," I said, nodding obediently, wiping away tears and hating myself for how obsequious I sounded. "I'll be so fast," I assured him.

I went into the booth, closed the door, and tried to calm myself down as I dialed. Maybe I had been the girl who cried when she couldn't talk to her boyfriend, but I didn't have to be the girl who called her boyfriend crying. No answer. A faucet had been turned on, and I couldn't turn it off. I was fully sobbing in the booth. I heard the *clunk* of the camera on the glass window.

"Fuck," I said under my breath, and tried to pull it together. I was sure this would be my defining moment and broadcast to millions of people (it didn't make it to air).

We had a list of people whom we were allowed to call that we'd submitted during the audition process. They'd all had to sign NDAs and contracts basically signing over all their life rights, so it wasn't a small ask. But my best friends had done it without a second thought. I dialed Michael's number.

"Hello?" he said.

A prerecorded message started playing: "This telephone call is being recorded for use in television broadcasting." *Click.*

"Hey, it's Sarah," I said when it was done, sniffling a little.

"Are you crying?"

"Yeah. I only have three minutes to talk, and Ian didn't pick up, and I really wanted to talk to him."

"Sarahhhhhhhhh," he said in that judgmental, sarcastic tone that is reserved for only the best of friends. "Are you being that girl?"

"Michael, I am absolutely being that girl!"

"Do you misssss me?" he said in a heavy Russian accent, imitating the contestant from the season we'd watched and mocked together. I laughed. I also felt a pang of guilt and self-awareness at acting exactly like the girl I'd made fun of so recently.

"Do you looooooove me?" I replied.

"So how is it?"

"It's . . . insane."

"Cool."

"Yeah."

And that was it: exactly what I needed. A little armor to carry me back into the fray.

Slowly, within the chaos and challenges of shooting the show, little eddies of routine and ease emerged. We were all surprised by how quickly we got used to the camera crews. The first few days we were changing our clothes hidden underneath a towel or inside the shower, jumping whenever we heard the *clomp clomp clomp* of six little feet in combat boots and Converse sneakers announcing the herd of camerapeople who would ambush us midconversation.

A week later I was clipping my toenails and moisturizing my feet in front of the mirror while the crew walked behind me to film some girls shaving their legs in the shower. None of us even looked up.

Although I quickly learned to ignore them, I still never knew what they would film. Once we were all huddled together, giggling and exchanging our deepest, darkest secrets, and there wasn't a *clomp, clomp,* or *clomp* to be heard. But you better believe when I was trimming those toenails, they were sure to capture it, getting so close I was afraid they'd get hit by a stray clipping.

The only consistent element was sleep deprivation. I asked Claire Unabia, who competed on Cycle 10 and who had an infant daughter at home while she was shooting, about how the sleep deprivation of the show compared to having a baby.

"Were you the only one who was sleeping more in the house than you had been at home?"

"No, honestly. When we were shooting, I felt like I did when my daughter was a newborn, just running on so little sleep, it was crazy. And just no schedule, no regularity ever."

It was so gratifying to hear. At the time, I was so disappointed in myself for feeling so run down all the time. I hated my body even more for feeling so weak and my brain for feeling so foggy. We were all drinking more caffeine than ever before.

And then, a few weeks in, we got a day off. A whole day to just hang out at the house. We were so excited. I stayed in bed for a few minutes after I woke up, relishing the luxury of having nowhere to be. Then I got up and got mic'd. Frank and I started our now normal routine.

"Hey, Frank. I'm Sarah."

"I know."

"Okay, but did you know that orca whales are actually the largest dolphins?"

"I did know that, actually."

"Twist!"

Later that day, it seemed only right to go skinny-dipping again. But for some reason, Jenah and I decided to race through the house naked together first beforehand. Then we put our bathing suits on in the water, which she did much faster than I, and she soon got a mischievous look in her eye.

"Don't even think about it," I said.

"I'm not. I won't."

Whip fast, she grabbed my bathing suit top away from me and ran, grabbing the towels as she went. I ran after her, giggling and screaming, but she was faster than I was and beat me inside, locking the screen door.

So not only did I have to walk upstairs to get in the house, but

I had to do it in front of the giant glass wall and transparent staircase, fully on display the whole time. I decided to turn this potential walk of shame into a strut of pride and did it with my arms above my head. When I'd walked upstairs, through the kitchen, and back downstairs, all topless, I went up to Jenah, put my leg up on her bed, and reached out for the towel.

"Yo," Bianca howled, "Sarah really does not give a fuck!"

I grinned. Then, as I walked away, I felt a pang of fear. Should I be giving a fuck? I'd never minded being naked or nearly naked in front of people before. Hell, I'd done it on stages and bars all over Boston. Somehow, despite all my issues with my body, exposing it felt safer than covering it up. I didn't have to wonder if everyone was thinking about it if it was out there for everyone to see. Furthermore, if my body was being perceived, it was easier to disassociate from it. It wasn't mine; it wasn't me. It was just a tool that I was using. But this was different. This was television. And I was pretty sure, as the plus-size contestant, I was supposed to be like the fat, funny friend, sitting on the sidelines while other people ran around naked.

Still, it felt good to have been uninhibited and free, even if just for a moment. Jenah and I were getting close enough that, occasionally, I felt like I could be myself, my preshow self, around her. She was a study in extremes: both soft and hard at once. Big, dreamy blue eyes with an intense stare that made me feel on the spot when she asked me questions. She was edgy and rock and roll and loved taking the piss, but she was also sweet and sensitive. Jenah and I (along with Janet) were also the only ones who had any idea how to cook. We'd both had to cook for our families as teenagers, which gave us an advantage. One morning, we taught a few of the other girls how to scramble eggs. Although we still struggled without a microwave; there wasn't a lot of time to spend on cooking, so we mostly got instant food that we either ate cold or figured out how to cook in the oven: Hot Pockets, frozen meals, frozen fries, granola bars.

Every day, a crew member would dole out thirty-seven dollars to each of us to spend on food. Then, every week, we were instructed to write out a list and leave it, along with all our cash, for someone to go grocery shopping for us. At the end of the day, there would be plastic bags with our change clipped to them. Substitutions would be at their discretion, and if the money didn't cover everything, omissions were at their discretion as well.

I was desperate to spend as little of my food stipend as possible. That was the only money we would be getting—we weren't being paid, and we wouldn't be getting residuals, so I wanted to make the most out of it. I stole as much as I could from craft services whenever I could. They usually fed us lunch on photo shoot days, and I would stuff bags of chips, sodas, and canned coffees into my pockets and purse.

Usually, we all ate our meals separately or on the go, but every once in a while, when there was time, we'd all sit down to dinner together. It was at one of these dinners that I first mentioned Lurlene. I can't remember how it came up, but Bianca loved her.

"Sarah, you make me giggle," she said. "Do Lurlene, do the voice."

"I don't know if I'm gon' find my baby daddy here, it's so fancy! Y'all think a man who hangs out in the back room of a 7-Eleven gon' be around here?"

I was really coming to love these girls, but I craved solitude. I was constantly trying to find ways to be alone.

I'd sit in a bathroom stall for so long the other girls probably thought I had chronic diarrhea or something. In one of the stalls, there was a television, which blew my mind. Who were the people who lived here normally? Who just went about their day, out in the world, after the incredible luxury of watching television in their tiny toilet room? There were other TVs in the house, but they'd all been disabled. One day, on a whim, I turned this bathroom TV on, and, much to my shock, it worked. Not only did it turn on, but it also had hundreds of channels. I almost laughed aloud, knowing that my imaginary chronic diarrhea was about to get *much* worse. I kept flipping through channels, and the last channel didn't look like any show or commercial I'd ever seen. It looked like security camera footage. I peered a little closer and realized it was the live feed from the cameras that were hidden all over the house. I felt a pit of excitement and nerves fall into my stomach. My mouth dropped open. I could see all the other girls, the crew, the entire house. I could even see people going through the door that had been disguised as a wall.

Man, I thought. *I wish I were an evil genius who knew what to do with this information.* As it was, I just sat and watched silent TV for way too long in that tiny stall.

The other thing I did to be alone was wash dishes. They'd probably removed the dishwasher to create conflict, but instead it just gave me an excuse to be in the kitchen when everyone was elsewhere. One day, I was doing the dishes, and suddenly I had three people close enough to me to feel their breath on my neck. I didn't want to look annoyed because I didn't want it to seem like I was mad about doing the dishes. So I held my face as neutrally as I could and tried to ignore them. Fifteen minutes later, they were still there, and I was struggling. Finally, I looked up and said, "How could this possibly be interesting?!"

The woman holding the camera looked up at me like I was a bug on her shoe. I swallowed guiltily. I knew I'd fucked up. "Do you know that you just ruined the entire shot?" she asked, and they all stomped away. I felt a hot mixture of anger, guilt, and adrenaline coursing through me.

Later on, in an interview, a producer asked me, "Isn't it annoying to be the only one who does dishes?"

"No, I like doing dishes," I said, blithely unaware that they were trying to stir up drama.

"But wouldn't it be nice if the other girls at least said thank you?"

"I don't care. I don't even know if they know that I'm doing them. I find it soothing."

They shrugged and gave up.

Every morning, no matter how early it meant getting up, I would try to sneak a swim in the pool. And when we got back at the end of the day, I would volunteer to be the last one in the confessional so I could sit in there and decompress as much as possible. Sometimes I'd go in there and read. Of course, I couldn't relax all the way, because I knew that there was someone on the other end of the camera. Some poor PA, probably, who had to suffer through watching me just sit there, reading or closing my eyes, basking in the pseudo-solitude.

The irony of being silent in the exact place where we were meant to confess our deepest, darkest secrets was not lost on me. But I've never been able to keep a secret. Except, apparently, from myself.

7

The Closet

In middle school, I started having dreams where I was a man having sex with a woman.

I dreamt about Leonardo DiCaprio last night . . . I dreamt that I was him in the car with Rose, and I made her hand slap the window, I wrote in my journal.

I thought it meant that I had such a crush . . . on the men. I wanted to *be* them.

I dreamt that I was Abby's boyfriend last night. I've never even met him! But he must be so hot because Abby is sooo pretty, I'm so jealous of her hair. I dreamt I/he and her were . . . you know . . . together.

Then I became a teenager and the dreams mostly faded as I toggled back and forth between wanting to be seen by men and wanting to be invisible. I was locked in power struggles with my parents, my teachers, the world, and it all seemed to revolve around how men thought of me. Being tall, young, and hot, I felt like I was on display every time I went in public and either loved or hated it, depending on the day, hour, minute.

Going on a reality show was like throwing a hot stone into an already boiling cauldron of soup. I was more visible than ever, but

I was also losing huge swaths of my personality. I wasn't becoming famous as myself; I was joining a famous pack of young women. We were all being manipulated and edited into portraying what some middle-aged producers wanted to show the world. The second I walked through the door of that bizarre mansion in the Hollywood Hills, I became a shaky, unwitting part of my own representation in the media.

At that point my queerness was just a festering secret that I could barely stand to look at, let alone reveal to anyone else. But it was there, fighting to get out, itching in the back of my brain, more and more every day. And now, here I was, stretched thin by lack of sleep and more on display than ever.

And I was locked in a new power struggle: us against the crew. They controlled when we ate, where we went, and when we were on camera. And we tried to undermine them without directly breaking the rules whenever we could. We were the younger siblings annoying our older siblings because we were too afraid to fight with our parents, the producers.

To challenge them, Kimberly Leemans recalled one instance when a few of us were hanging out on the patio with the cameras on us. "I guess we were boring, so they went off to go find the other girls. And then I just remember fake punching my wrist, before yelling, 'You bitch, get off me!' Then they ran in to find us just picking at our nails, and they were like, 'You can't do that.'" Kim taunted them further, asking, "Do what? Do what?"

Outside of the house, our producer-parents were in charge, and they ran a tight ship. At our first photo shoot, we walked onto the set to find Mr. Jay, who laid out the theme: smoking. We'd be doing glamorous "before" and grim "after" shots to show the tragic side effects of smoking. I was premature aging, the horror. The second they called cut on Mr. Jay's segment, a cavalcade of PAs rushed in with clipboards and earpieces to divide us up and bring us to either hair and makeup, the stylists, or holding, which was where I was going.

As they walked us back into yet another windowless room, I sighed, assuming we'd have to sit in silence again. But to my surprise, a camera crew parked themselves in the corner, and we were allowed to talk! So, of course, my nerves got the best of me, and I clammed up and was too nervous to say anything. I sat, watching the other girls chat among themselves about their plans for when they got on set to take pictures.

Eventually I was taken to hair and makeup, which, yet again, felt like a warm respite. And not just because the light was literally warmer, but also because hair and makeup was a little queer haven. Of course, not everyone was gay, but anyone who wasn't got labeled as such: "That's Christian; he's in charge of hair. He's straight, but we love him anyway."

Sutan Amrull, also known as Raja and the future winner of season three of *RuPaul's Drag Race,* was the head makeup artist, and they introduced themselves and got to work on my face. Sutan was the most beautiful person I'd ever seen: tall and lean with gleaming skin and long, dark, shiny hair. I asked them about themselves and was so excited to learn that they were a drag queen.

I've been obsessed with drag queens since I was six years old and watched RuPaul's Christmas special on VHS. I watched it until the tape got wonky, imitating Ru and La Toya Jackson. My mom snuck me into a drag bar when I was sixteen as a Christmas present. A drag queen stuck my head up her skirt, and it was the best day of my life.

"Do you have any pictures?" I demanded.

"I do," Sutan said with a laugh.

"Can I see them?!" I asked with an unseemly intensity.

"Maybe I'll bring them sometime."

I always left hair and makeup less nervous than when I walked in, not least because I looked magnitudes better, but also because, in there, my brain could quiet itself to focus on the fascinating person painting my face, transforming me into someone better, prettier, more like a drag queen.

After makeup, it was time for styling. The stylists were two terrifying, tiny, and very similar looking women named Anda and Masha, the embodiment of LA cool, who always wore all black, accessorized with tasteful oversize silver jewelry. They would look us up and down, purse their lips, sigh, and pull inspiration from the sky and clothes off the rack.

They walked me past the racks of size twos and zeros to a separate section and put me in a beautiful Dolce & Gabbana leopard-print bra, a slip of a nightgown, and some '50s-style nude pumps.

"How much do these shoes cost?" I asked Anda or maybe Masha.

"Probably eight hundred, nine hundred dollars," one replied. "They're on loan."

"That's more than my grandmother's engagement ring," I said.

"You look hot, girl," said Anda or possibly Masha.

"So hot," agreed Masha or possibly Anda. "Very pinup."

I looked down at myself in the outfit and was surprised to find that it didn't feel any different from the cheap, regular clothes I'd come in. Of course it was beautiful, but it hadn't turned me into a different person. I was still me, and I was still nervous. I walked to the set, and the photographer, Mike Rosenthal, was sitting with his camera looking disinterested. He barely looked at me as I approached. Mr. Jay had been showing someone his new iPhone and all the features as I walked up. He rolled his eyes as he put it in his pocket and took a deep, ragged sigh as though he were steeling himself to be on camera again. I went to the boudoir stool in the center of the set and tried to keep breathing myself. Mr. Jay rubbed his temples. I swallowed nervously and steeled myself. This felt different from the shoot in the warehouse, just a few days ago now. This one *counted*.

"Okay, Sarah, let's do this," said Mr. Jay.

I sat nervously on the tiny stool and looked at Mr. Jay and then at the camera. I moved my body like I thought a pinup girl would.

"Okay," purred Mr. Jay. "She's posing down to her toes, I love that."

I looked at him. He was looking at me. So was Mike Rosenthal. So was the camera crew. I felt flush with excitement and embarrassment. I looked down at my toes. They were pointed, in the elegant heels, at the end of my leg, which looked longer than I remembered. Here it was. The moment I'd been waiting for. I didn't know if it was the clothes, or the set, or all the concentrated, unfiltered attention, but suddenly I *did* feel like a different person. I wasn't nervous. I was a classy, sophisticated *woman*. I kept posing, moving every time the camera clicked. I felt incredible. After years of disassociating when I needed to feel safe, here was a way to be completely present and aware of my head to my toes, while also compartmentalizing any emotions about it.

It wasn't completely without hiccups. I was still a beginner, after all.

"Can I move my hands?" I asked, bringing them up to touch my chin.

"Not if you're going to do *that* with them," replied Mr. Jay.

That might have hurt my feelings in the real world, but in front of the camera, I didn't care. My body wasn't mine anymore, it was a product. It was doing its job. I softened my hands.

"Better," said Mr. Jay.

I walked off set and went to sit with the other girls, feeling almost high. By the time my butt hit the chair, my old self had come rushing back. I was nervous, detached. Damn. A PA came to take me to do what they called an OTF—on the fly—interview to capture my thoughts in the moment.

"How did it go?" asked the producer.

"The shoot went really well; it was so much fun!" I replied confidently. "Surprisingly well! I mean, I don't know. I think it did." I was losing steam.

"Was it hard to be the only plus-size girl on set when all the other girls are so much thinner?"

"Oh." I deflated. "I hadn't really thought about it." But I hadn't included their question in my answer like we were supposed to. "It wasn't really that hard to be the only plus-size girl on set," I reiterated. "I didn't really think about it that much, but I guess maybe we'll see at judging. I hope I did well."

"Do you think you have to work harder than the other girls because you're plus-size? To prove something?"

"I don't know if I have to work harder because I'm plus-size. In the moment, on set, I was just kind of in a zone, you know? So I didn't think about it. But I guess maybe I should work harder, because I'm not . . . I'm not like the other girls."

"What was it like when you didn't have as many clothing options as the other girls? Because they're all sample size."

"What's 'sample size'?"

"When designers send clothes to models or celebrities to wear or when they have clothes for a runway show, they're all a size two, so it's called 'sample size.' It's, like, the standard."

All my steam was gone now. I thought back to getting dressed with Anda and Masha and the tiny, separate section they'd had to choose from. My brain started tainting the memory. *They were lying when they said you were hot,* I told myself. *They meant you were hot for a fat girl. You can't be a model. You can't even wear de-signer clothes; you just get a nightgown.* I swallowed and looked around, trying to figure out how to work their original question into my answer.

"The stylists had fewer clothes for me than for the other girls, which I guess makes sense. I don't know, I hadn't really noticed that until just now. They did a great job, though! I really liked what they had for me to wear."

I could tell that wasn't what they wanted to hear. Was I sup-posed to be sad? Or somehow confident? Was I supposed to be mad at the stylists? That didn't seem right. None of it felt right.

THE FOLLOWING DAY, the crew members wrangled us all into the outdoor sitting area. We were idly chatting when in walked Miss J wearing a tasteful blazer and an argyle sweater over a button-down shirt with a big, exaggerated collar. They looked like a fashion sketch version of a professor. She outlined what kinds of basics we would need to be a model. Specifically, for castings, every model should have nude thongs, plain black tank tops, black heels, and dark skinny jeans, to keep our style pared down and classy but still show off who we were.

"Cut!" called the director.

Then they told us Miss J was going to give us a piece of news and we had to have *big* reactions.

"You guys are going to Old Navy . . ." she revealed, while a crew member gestured to us to scream with glee, which we did. ". . . to pick some basic items that you girls need to impress us when you come in to judging," continued Miss J. They filmed his "exit," but he came back afterward.

"How are you all doing in the house?" asked Miss J. He stayed and listened to all our answers.

"Our first teach!" said Saleisha once they were gone.

I blushed, hoping I had absorbed all of Miss J's advice: I hadn't even realized it was a teach.

SHORTLY AFTER THAT, they herded us into the van and drove us to what turned out to be a mall. They hurried us inside the cavernous, empty Old Navy because apparently there were paparazzi outside trying to get a picture of all of us. The crew was annoyed. I was delighted. Paparazzi! We waited while the crew made sure to block all the store's windows and got set up.

We stood expectantly, and then Benny Ninja, a vogue dancer and head of the House of Ninja, one of the major houses in the New York City ballroom scene, appeared.

He told us we were about to have our first challenge—a fashion challenge. We were to run around the store and assemble an outfit fit for a model. He counted us down, and we took off, running frantically around the store grabbing as much as we could. I had no idea what jeans size I was, so I grabbed a skirt.

"More glamour! More accessories!" Benny kept yelling. He'd show up behind us and say, "More! Bigger! Make a splash!" He personally was wearing at least twelve scarves. I grabbed a necklace and some high heels and hoped they were enough.

THEN CAME OUR first elimination. Or, at least, we were pretty sure that's what it was. We were brought to a soundstage early in the morning. A handler walked us all the way to the very back, had us file into a windowless room, and put us on ice. The room was tastefully decorated, with giant white couches and fake flowers. After what felt like hours, they brought us to set to do light and sound tests, and we saw the iconic stage. There was a table on one end where the judges sat and a long runway and a platform for us to stand on. It felt like a whole different world from the rest of the building, which was cement floors and walls, with bulky film equipment everywhere.

One of the crew members, a man named JB, who looked like a leaner, tattooed Jack Black and whom we'd all come to like, came up to prep us for the day.

"Listen, I'm going to be real with you: this is going to be a long day. Last cycle, a girl collapsed at almost every elimination, but we are going to avoid that, right?"

We looked at him, aghast.

"Do not lock your knees," he told us. "That's the most important thing. You're going to be standing for a long time, and it cuts off the blood flow and can knock you out. And be sure to eat when we break for lunch and drink plenty of water. If you feel faint, raise your hand. Don't be a hero. Raise your hand and someone will come help you. Do not worry about getting in trouble or interrupting, okay? Even if we're filming, if you feel faint, raise your hand, and someone will come help you. Take care of yourselves."

I rolled my eyes. *These skinny bitches*, I thought. *Can't even stand around. How hard is that?!*

I was bursting with energy as they positioned us on the platform facing the judges. Like she would every week, Tyra told us the prizes: a contract with Elite Model Management, a seven-page spread in *Seventeen* magazine, and a $100,000 contract with CoverGirl cosmetics. As always, she was perfectly made up and had her on-camera face on—composed and hiding any inkling of how she was really feeling. I'd known performers who could turn it on like her, but I'd never met someone who never seemed to turn it off. I couldn't see any chinks in her armor, no matter how long I looked.

Then she introduced the judges, but I already knew all their names by heart. Nigel Barker, noted fashion photographer, a tall, slender British man with a perfectly styled five o'clock shadow. Miss J, runway coach diva extraordinaire. She sat pertly to Tyra's right, a one-inch Afro wig on her head. And lastly, Twiggy, one of the first and most iconic supermodels, a blond British woman with famously big blue eyes who smiled sweetly and waved at all of us.

Then they called us up one by one and critiqued our outfit from the Old Navy challenge as well as our photo from the anti-smoking shoot. I was surprised at how much feedback each girl got, at least half an hour, often having to pause to fix lighting or reshoot a particular moment.

The judges immediately hated the necklace I had chosen, which Miss J called a noose.

"It was an awkward length, so I tried to tie it up," I explained.

"Oh, just take the damn thing off," Miss J said with her signature sass.

"Now that's a model outfit," said Tyra, of my red tank top and jean skirt.

"Yes, you have beautiful legs, if a little thick. Well, a lot thick," said Twiggy.

"Her legs look like mine, girl!" said Tyra.

I couldn't stop grinning. I couldn't believe this was real. Twiggy could say whatever she wanted about my legs if it meant they looked like Tyra's.

Then they looked at my photo and my legs came up again. "Look at the angles in your leg," said Nigel. "That's quite artful, really."

"Yeah," agreed Tyra. "Mr. Jay said she was posing down to her toes, and I agree. Looking through your film, I could tell. This is well done."

When they sent me back to the line, I was dizzy with excitement. And then I was just plain old dizzy. My snark about those skinny bitches not being able to stand around came back to haunt me, swimming in front of my eyes along with everything else. I was covered in sweat. I started to keel over. I thought about how JB said not to worry about interrupting filming, but I worried. They were about to announce the winner of the challenge, and I couldn't bear to draw out that suspense any longer than they already were.

I managed to hold on until they announced that Saleisha had won the Old Navy fashion challenge, although when they told us to cheer for Old Navy again, I could barely muster a "Woo!" Finally, someone called cut, and I slumped to the floor. A PA rushed over with Gatorade and had me sit down and put my head between my knees.

"I'm so sorry," I said.

"Drink this," she replied.

I drank it.

"Are you okay now? Do you think you're gonna go down?"

"I'm fine, I'm okay."

"Do you need help getting up?"

"No, no, I'm okay."

I started to stand and quickly realized I was wrong. I stumbled, and the PA put my arm around her shoulders. I sat back down for a few minutes, and only then did I have a chance to be disappointed with how I'd done in the challenge.

Saleisha had been smart and listened to Miss J when she went about picking her outfit in Old Navy. She picked a simple, classic outfit, whereas the rest of us had listened to Benny Ninja and accessorized heavily, trying to create glamorous looks. I made a note to try to prioritize whatever the judges said above all else.

Eventually, I felt well enough to stand, and we finished filming the judging. We all trooped offstage, stepping down from the fantasy world of the elimination set back into the real world: a dark, windowless soundstage where we had to sit in silence. We were back on ice while the judges deliberated.

"Can we have our iPods?"

"No."

"Can we have our books?"

"No."

After a few hours of sitting with our thoughts, they brought us back out. A bunch of us had fallen asleep, and there was a post-nap fog over our eyes. But mine still went straight to Tyra.

"We're taking a stand," she was saying. "This is a no-smoking cycle. So many young girls are fans of *America's Next Top Model,* and right now, so many girls are fans of you. So, if they see their idol puffing and smoking a cigarette, what does that make them think? *Wow, she's smoking? That's cool.* So that's why smoking will be banned. As of tomorrow. You want to smoke tonight? Get your last puffs, and then it's over."

I thought of the carton of cigarettes sitting in the closet back at the house. I thought about the dollars I'd scraped and stolen from my mom to buy it and was ashamed. And annoyed.

ELIMINATION DAYS ALWAYS made me feel like I was on a tight leash. In addition to the tension of wondering who was going home, we couldn't move around or do anything to release it. There was no acting out here. And now, in addition to being constrained and controlled all day, we were also in nicotine withdrawal. Emotions ran high. Tempers ran short. But most of the time, the girls and I were a unified front fighting against the powers that be: the crew.

Although we couldn't really break the rules. The house was

the closest thing we had to a home field advantage, and there was nowhere to sneak anything, let alone a cigarette. But we did have ways of subtly fighting back. When we wanted to ensure certain moments didn't make it to air, we'd sing famous songs or mention brands or Disney characters.

"Sarah. Sarah. Help me. Take the wheel. Explain Asperger's to me again. Heather is on my last nerve," said Janet, and immediately we heard the *clomp clomp clomp* of the approaching crew.

"Hakuna matata," I sang, "it's like autism. Hakuna matata, it means she can't read . . ." The tune was running out, so I had to say this last part super fast. ". . . facial cues like other people."

"Okay, so, she can't tell when we're upset and stuff?" she asked, to the tune of the McDonald's "I'm Lovin' It" jingle. "Is that right?"

"Yeah," I answered normally. "Just be really extra clear about everything."

"Got it, got it," said Janet. "That's easy. Hell, we should all be like Heather. Ba-da-ba-ba-ba, I'm lovin' it."

We realized soon after moving in that the sound of the jets in the hot tub made it hard to hear us on camera. Because we couldn't keep the mic packs on in the water, the crew would have to use the much heavier and more unwieldy boom mics to manually follow our sound, which isn't easy in an unscripted show. Not only would they have to hold that big, heavy piece of equipment over our heads, but they were also standing over a big, steamy bowl of model soup. We started spending a lot of time there, me most of all. If I wasn't in bed or doing an interview, I was going back and forth between the pool and the hot tub.

Then, for a while, they banned us from the hot tub. I was furious. I'd stare at it longingly and pout and say passive-aggressive things into my mic about it. Whenever I used the bathroom, I would whisper into my mic so the sound guys didn't hear anything else. I started with more whale and shark facts, but now that I wasn't allowed in the hot tub, I would complain about that. "Gosh, I really feel like confessing a super-juicy secret, but only if I could be soaking in some warm water," I'd hiss.

After the hot tub, we started hanging out in the bathroom, thinking they wouldn't want to film there. But the bathroom was full of security cameras, so we'd actually made the crew's life much easier. They kept outsmarting us at every move, until we started hanging out in the closet. They could still film us in there, but not only could we hear them coming, but they also couldn't get super close to us.

Whenever we had a few free hours, which didn't happen often, we almost always ended up sitting in a circle on the floor telling secrets and stories, snacking, and hiding from our "parents" like it was a middle school sleepover. Although I'd known the girls in the house only for a few weeks, they were literally the only other people in the world who could relate to what I was going through. We were in the process of changing our lives, and that change was going to be on display to millions of people. Sometimes it felt like the other girls were the only witnesses I could trust.

Jenah and I bonded over the fact that we both did theater in high school.

"I'm probably a better actor than you," she joked.

I stared stone-faced back at her. We both broke at the same time, bending over with laughter.

"Kidding, kidding," she said, poking me gently.

Heather and I bonded over wanting to be cool and rebellious but being people pleasers at heart. We couldn't wait for the makeovers; we both hoped they'd chop off all our hair so we could be as edgy as we felt.

Jenah, Janet, and I all bonded over having to quit smoking cold turkey. The first week, our bodies were a mess.

"I didn't even smoke that much!" complained Janet one morning as we drank our coffee, without our usual smokes.

"Me neither!" I said.

"I did," said Jenah, which was true.

"But it's good. It's good for us," said Janet, and we all nodded, grumpy and jittery.

There were cliques and momentary tiffs or rivalries, but overall, it felt like camp. We were all in for this wild ride. According to Dr. Molly Millwood, in her book *To Have and to Hold: Motherhood, Marriage, and the Modern Dilemma,* "When two (or more) women who know and trust each other simply spend time together, they experience increases in oxytocin, which in turn increase feelings of empathy and fondness for one another and decrease cortisol, which is the stress hormone." So maybe, as we sat in a circle, strangers becoming something like friends, we were clinging to a sense of warmth and community in the face of all the chaos, seeing one another as we wanted to be seen.

We talked about everything: ambitions, creative desires, sex. And since I would never share any of their stories, I can only tell you my own contributions. One was about the time I hooked up with a (semi)professional skateboarder in his dingy bathroom while my best friend and his roommate sat in their equally dingy living room and tried to pretend they didn't know what was happening in the next room.

One day, Lisa casually mentioned that she was bisexual. I forget how it even came up, but once it was out in the air, there was a bit of a pause as everyone reacted and she basked in the glow of our attention, a catlike smile on her face.

"Does the show know that?" asked one girl, incredulous.

"I think so. I've always been very open about it."

"Are any of us your type?" someone else asked her.

"Oh yeah," she said, without elaborating.

I felt a thrill run up my spine. I looked around. I wasn't attracted to Lisa or any of the other girls. None of them were *my* type. But all of a sudden, I was unable to ignore the fact that . . . I did have a type. There was, in fact, a type of woman I was attracted to. Many types.

Of course, I knew that on some level because I'd hooked up with a woman the year before. But I had so much shame around it that I'd brushed it off as a one-time thing that happened three times and never really let the thought condense in my mind: *I am attracted to women.* This conversation was electrifying. It felt like when *The Wizard of Oz* suddenly switches to Technicolor.

I GREW UP in one of the most liberal places in the country. Homosexuality was never something that had to be explained to me when I was a kid; it was just one of the natural paths of life that I saw around me. When I was three, our landlords were a gay couple. The postmaster of our town was a trans woman. But remote as it was, I wasn't totally removed from popular culture and biases. I still heard jokes and comments about how greedy and indecisive bisexual people were. My freshman year of college, I watched a rerun of *Sex and the City* on TBS where all the characters agreed that bisexual men were gay and bisexual women were only doing it for attention. And everyone knows there's nothing worse than a woman asking for attention.

When I was fourteen, my grandparents and I happened across the gay pride parade in Montreal. We walked out of the Montreal Museum of Fine Arts and there it was. So rather than navigate our way through, we hunkered down on the steps and watched the floats pass by. Truck platforms with mostly shirtless men waving. Biker gangs of thick, tattooed women. Shiny corporate floats sponsored by Citibank or various liquor companies. One of the liquor-sponsored floats was throwing tiny bottles of booze into the crowd. I went to grab one.

"Don't even think about it," said my grandfather. "I'll be in enough trouble for that Coke."

I sipped my soda and pouted. It was hot, and my hair was sticking to the back of my neck and getting tangled in my Deb halter top. My grandmother had warned me that my Old Navy flip-flops would not be good walking shoes, and she was right. A hot, angry blister was forming between my toes.

Then came a float of drag queens. Big everything: hair, heels, boobs, feather boas of all colors. It was enough to force me out of my teenage sulk and into a big, childlike grin. I waved and screamed like they were my favorite celebrities.

A few days later I was recounting everything to my dad in the car. "And there was a whole float of drag queens that were all dressed up as Disney princesses!"

"Yeah," said my dad, "most gay men are pretty degenerate."

I was stunned into silence. My parents are liberal hippies. The smell of the food co-ops they shopped at is burned into my memory's scent bank: tahini, patchouli, and body odor barely masked by natural deodorant. My mom had a COEXIST bumper sticker on her Subaru. They both had gay friends. My dad had multiple gay couples as roommates over the years.

"What about Quincy?" I said, one of his closest friends.

"Look, I love your uncle Quincy, but the things he does are pretty disgusting. I mean, just . . . sex all the time. Men are naturally depraved, so when you don't need women to have sex, it's just constant. And then that's why most lesbian couples never have sex. You need the balance."

I suddenly felt quite off-balance. I didn't want to know that about Quincy (who, by the way, is not my uncle). And I knew that wasn't true about lesbian couples, because just five years earlier, I'd walked in on two of our roommates having sex, a couple named Rachel and Louise. They were sweet and friendly and talked to me like I was an adult even though they were *so old* (they were probably in their early twenties). I felt so comfortable around them that one day I forgot to knock and barged through their door to Louise's bare legs twisting and writhing on their sheets. Rachel was mostly hidden under their paisley tapestry covers.

"Sorry!" I yelled, and ran out. Later we all three laughed about it, they got a lock installed, and I promised to always knock. That funny, treasured memory felt tainted now.

Like most teenagers, I was in the middle of confusing, painful, hormonal introspection. Distinguishing myself from my parents. Peeling away what I'd been raised with, layer by layer, and holding it out and examining it in the light. And I felt myself pulling away from my dad and everyone else. There was no light by which to examine this layer, so I just hid it away.

Then I got to college and discovered it was the hot, cool-girl thing to make out with one another while guys watched and cheered us on. It filled me with a rage I didn't understand. I hated the men who watched, I hated that my friends wanted to do it, and, most of all, I hated myself for playing along. I didn't understand why I couldn't find the strength to just say no.

But, then again, I didn't know how to say no to much of anything. I was overwhelmed by everything in college, good and bad. During orientation, our overly perky tour guide mentioned that there were more than a thousand cardio machines at the main gym on campus. *That's more than all the people in my town,* I thought. *Everyone and their dogs could exercise at the same time.* It was the first time I had access to the food I wanted, the drinks I wanted, and the people I wanted. And the people I didn't want but didn't know how to say no to. If I couldn't make up an excuse or run away or use my friends as cover, I found myself sleeping with men, whether I wanted to or not. Sex went from something I wanted, something I pursued with my high school boyfriends, to something that I agreed to, was coerced into, or couldn't escape. Except by disassociating. I'd lie there and let the hazy, familiar feeling wash over me, greeting it like an old friend. Stare at the ceiling or the floor and enjoy the cavernous silence in my mind. Afterward, I'd feel like I'd lost something, but I couldn't put my finger on what. It was too painful to focus on, so I kept it blurry.

In the rare moments of clarity, I found myself wondering if maybe, after everything, I was a lesbian. But I had to admit, I was attracted to men. I was still deep in denial about there being a third option, even when I kissed a waitress outside the diner she worked at. Even when I went home with her and found myself present for the first time, which meant being open and vulnerable in a way I never had before. Afterward, I snapped shut like a spring-loaded clamshell, hard and angry and cruel.

I told her and myself that it didn't mean anything, but I knew that wasn't true when I kept it a secret from Meredith and Michael. I didn't know how to explain any of it.

It's just because she's so butch, I thought, *that's why I was attracted to her.*

And then when I began working with the burlesque troupe, I developed an obsession with a high-femme dancer. I convinced myself I just wanted to be like her. And I hated when she would tell us about the various people she was dating because I didn't think they were good enough for her. I barely knew her, but I wanted to be her only friend, to follow her around like a puppy—which I did, every time I was around her. And then, when she kissed me, I pushed her away and accused her of using me to get attention. Hard and angry and cruel.

A FEW DAYS after my Technicolor awakening, Jenah and I were sitting in the closet in silence, trying to be alone together. Suddenly, without any warning to her or, honestly, to myself, I found myself saying, "Did you hear that Lisa is bi?"

"Oh," said Jenah, "so am I."

My mouth was dry and my mind was spinning as I did my best not to show it. "You are? Like . . . you are . . . you have . . ." I was sputtering.

"Like, I have been with men and then I have also been with women, yes," she said, patient but a little confused by my reaction.

"When you were with women, was it . . . was it for real or for sex?"

She looked at me, unsure how to answer. "For . . . real? I mean, we had sex, but, like, we also dated."

"Huh," I said. "I am too. But I've never dated a woman. Just been, you know, with them . . . like for sex. I wanted to, though."

"Cool," she said.

I felt like a kid who just got away with something. Suddenly, it seemed so obvious: *I am bisexual.* I was honestly a little embarrassed that it had never occurred to me before. I stifled a rueful laugh. Had I just come out of the closet? I looked nervously at the man holding a camera about six feet away. Had I just come out of the closet on national fucking television? Had I just come out of the closet . . . while sitting in a literal closet?

"Don't look at the camera," the camera guy said. I took my wide eyes elsewhere, still trying my hardest to look cool.

After all that, my big moment didn't even make it to air. None of the bisexual conversations did. But that didn't really matter. I didn't need it to be on television to make a difference. I'd finally articulated something that had been wafting around in my brain for years.

I don't know what shifted and made me come out on the show. Maybe it was trauma bonding. Maybe it was because I was surrounded only by women, two of whom happened to be queer. And despite the fact that, in reality, we were hypervisible, in those moments it felt as though we were safely ensconced from the male gaze in this artificial world.

Turns out my "safe space" was the floor of a walk-in closet in a mansion in the Hollywood Hills.

8

Out of
My Head

"Loosen up," my high school theater director had said as I stood in the middle of the auditorium. "You're in your head."

"Where else would I be?" I asked. "Where are you?"

"In my body. You need to be in your body."

I looked down at the terrifying cesspool of my physical form. *Surely not,* I thought. *That's not a safe place to be.*

Now photo shoots had shown me a place where I could safely be present for the first time. But the rest of the time we were filming, I felt like I was floating, watching myself go through the motions of being on a television show.

Our second challenge would be judged by a man named Roy Campbell and a designer named Colleen Quen. It was a runway show wearing Quen's couture gowns, which were stunning, dramatic, and comically difficult to walk in. There was one that had a train in the back *and* the front, one like a four-layer cake but each layer moved independently, and one that had big, heavy sleeves that dragged on the floor. The show took place in yet another hotel ballroom, with room dividers sectioning off the backstage.

Even after talking to Tara on the cruise ship, I still couldn't quite believe that I could ever do runway. It was too hard for me to conceptualize breaking the mold when I barely understood what it contained. When we got backstage at the runway challenge, I looked at all the elaborate sample-size dresses and wondered how the hell I would ever fit in one.

The answer? Elbow grease, safety pins, and prayer. The backstage coordinator let it slip that there was only one dress that could possibly be contorted to fit my body: a strapless minidress with a voluminous, ruffled overcoat that I was to use to hide the fashion Frankenstein back. Ebony had the same outfit in a different color: hers was gold, mine was maroon. The only difference was she was able to remove her top layer, revealing the perfectly fitted tube dress underneath.

My inner monologue all day was a constant stream of bile: *You are disgustingly fat and it is causing problems for everyone. The whole point of a runway show is to show off the clothes, and you can't even do that. You don't belong here. Even if you were thin, you wouldn't belong here. At best, the audience will pity you.*

On top of that, I was embarrassed that something as simple as walking back and forth was devastating me like this. I hated myself for hating myself. It felt so silly and stupid and important and all-consuming. I was stuck in a self-loathing spiral. The lens of my mental camera was stuck: I couldn't zoom out to get any sense of perspective.

The hair and makeup team was different from the regular crew this week.

"You have, like, the perfect face," said my makeup artist. I peered up at her and then into the mirror, desperately trying to see myself through her eyes.

"Thank you so much," I said. I took her compliment, carefully folded it up, and held it close. It was enough to keep me going. The energy backstage was frantic, and I looked around, realizing that this was my first real fashion show. And I was a part of it. Gratitude wiggled its way through all my self-loathing, and I had to admit, I was so lucky to be here. I heard Roy onstage, describing all the dresses as the other girls walked down the runway.

"Imagine molten lava poured over your body," he intoned over Jenah's runway walk, "and there you have this curvaceous gown."

"You know the saying 'float like a butterfly, sting like a bee'? We went back to nature," he said while Saleisha was out there. He sounded just like the announcers from the fashion shows in old movies I loved, like *Cover Girl, Singin' in the Rain,* and *How to Marry a Millionaire,* so I assumed that all fashion shows had narrators.

After my makeup was done, an assistant came to help me into my shoes, and the second my toes hit the sole, I knew something was wrong.

"I'm so sorry, I don't think these are my size. I'm a ten," I lied. I'm an eleven.

We looked. They were size nine.

"There's nothing we can do now; you just have to make it work," the handler told me.

I scrunched up my toes as much as I could and teetered toward the runway to wait my turn. Victoria was ahead of me, and she was struggling too. She *hated* high heels.

"Do yours fit?" I asked. "Mine are two sizes too small."

"Are you serious?" she said, looking down at my cramped feet. "How are you even standing? Can't we get someone to fix this?"

I appreciated the concern, but this was the one good thing about disassociating: your feet can't hurt if you don't feel them.

The line of models shifted, and it was my turn. Someone helped me up the stairs, and the second my size nine heel hit the top step, I entered a fugue state. I have no memory of walking the runway.

Stepping into the offstage area felt like waking up. *Hello,* said my feet. *Welcome back. We are in pain.* I hobbled down the stairs, and a producer pulled me away for an OTF interview.

"How do you feel about Ebony almost running into you?" he asked me.

"What?" I said, clueless.

Apparently, Ebony and I had collided on my way back up the runway, and I somehow hadn't even noticed. Not a drop of alcohol, and this was the closest to blacking out I'd ever come. Fashion is a hell of a drug.

"I . . . Ebony ran into me? I don't think I even noticed when Ebony ran into me," I stammered, being sure to include the question in my confused answer. Had she really? I felt like surely it had been my fault somehow; I'd been so out of it—how could it not be? But the producer seemed pretty sure that it was she who had run into me. He explained what had happened and asked me to relay that back to camera.

"I guess . . . Ebony and I had sort of a hit-and-run," I said, gesturing with my hands, mirroring what the producer had described to me. "But it couldn't have been much of a bump. Maybe we were just too close to the middle."

"Do you think it was because you're plus-size, because you took up more of the runway?"

My heart sank. I had thought so many terrible things about myself, only to be blindsided by something I'd never even thought to be insecure about. Of course a model would run into me. I didn't even belong up there. The runway had rejected me like a body rejects a bad organ.

"I mean, it's very *Sex and the City,* right? I'm basically Carrie Bradshaw, is what I'm hearing," I said to camera, desperate to hide the spiral I was in.

During judging, Colleen Quen said my walk was fine but not

great, and Roy Campbell didn't give me any negative feedback, instead focusing on Ebony running into me. He even implied that it was on purpose. I knew there was no way that was true, but I still hoped, with a guilty pang, that her mistake would cost her. Anything to take the focus away from me.

As we were being judged, I realized that Mila, who had just been eliminated, had also walked in the runway and was undressing before being hurried off set.

Huh, I thought.

THE NEXT DAY, when we walked into our second photo shoot, I was nervous but hopeful: I'd been good at this last time. This week we'd be wearing designer dresses, heels . . . and rock-climbing harnesses: we would be posing at the top of a rock-climbing wall.

They sent us to hair and makeup, where they gave us elaborate, artistic, abstract makeup. Victoria said she felt like a "sea nymph on acid scaling the wall in the sunshine," and honestly? That's exactly what we looked like. I loved it. I felt magical. And Sutan brought pictures from their drag portfolio to show me. The makeup room, yet again, felt like a little haven inside the hectic climbing gym. I felt myself coming back down to earth a little . . .

. . . just in time to be hiked up a wall by some burly rock-climbing instructors.

"Sorry, I'm the heavy load," I joked, convinced that I was heavier than both of them. Heavier than anyone they'd ever taught rock climbing. Heavier than anyone in the world. They reassured me they'd hiked much heavier people up the wall, but I was still bracing myself. Were the producers going to ask me about this later? If something went wrong, it would be my fault for being heavier. I tried to shake it off, but all the noise and stimulation of the climbing equipment made it hard to get in the zone.

The photographer, Matthew Jordan Smith, could tell that something was off. "Just let it go," he told me. "Don't worry about the harness, just try to do something fun with your body."

His smile was grounding and kind and put me at ease. He even got a grin out of Mr. Jay. I took a deep breath and started swaying back and forth, moving my limbs around, and then bringing my eyes up to meet the camera. It was working. I could feel myself entering into that focused, calm mindset.

"Yes!" said Roy.

"Now she's getting it!" said Mr. Jay.

What the hell? I thought, and flipped myself upside down.

"Okay, your face?" said Mr. Jay. "Not good. You look terrible upside down—that's something for you to remember going forward."

"You still look stunning," the photographer reassured me. "It just doesn't photograph well when you're upside down."

I flipped back and kept it right side up for the rest of the shoot.

When they brought me down from the wall, it felt like coming down from a high. It had been so nice to get out of my head, but there was a mental hangover waiting for me when I landed. Had it been enough? What was going to happen at elimination? What were they going to say?

"This is a really skillful photograph, Sarah," said Nigel Barker, a photographer himself, at the next judging. I grinned, relief washing over me.

"The camera loves your face," said Tyra.

"It's true," agreed Twiggy. "In this photo you look stunning, which is surprising, to be honest, because in person you're quite plain."

She smiled jauntily at me and I smiled back. Her accent and her doll-like eyes always made me wonder if I was hearing her correctly. I was.

"Sarah, can you walk forward and back for me?" asked Tyra. As I walked up and down the runway, she looked me up and down and said, "Is there something wrong with your back?"

This was more than just panel feedback. This was special. I wanted to bask in Tyra's attention forever and never let it go. Say what you will about Tyra, but she is one of the most magnetic and compelling people I've ever met. Her gaze felt like the sun.

Granted, we were in the world she created, so of course she was the sun, the moon, the terrifying and mysterious universe. And now she was talking to me. And asking me a question. Which I was taking a really long time to answer. Like, uncomfortably long. *Say something, Sarah. Answer the question. Tell her that you have scoliosis. That in fifth grade, after the gym teacher ran his finger up and down all the kids' spines, he stopped at yours and told your parents to take you to a chiropractor, who did x-rays and found out that your spine is crooked. This is the kind of thing that reality shows love. Just say it, Sarah.* The judges were looking at me expectantly. What was this feeling? *Jesus, say anything, Sarah.*

"I . . . don't know," I stuttered.

"I think we need to get to the bottom of this," said Tyra. "Can we get her to a chiropractor to figure out what's going on with her back? Let's see if we can get you walking better."

"Yes, thank you," I said nervously.

I walked back to the line of girls dejected. Heather squeezed my arm as I walked by. Yet again, I had failed to be a compelling reality TV star with a catchy, fun, aesthetically pleasing illness. Instead, I was just an awkward girl who walked funny.

I'd forgotten to put the scoliosis on my medical history forms in the application. Was I going to get in trouble for not including it? Why had I frozen like that? What was that feeling? These were the questions rattling around in my head when Tyra told us the judges were going to deliberate and decide who would continue on in the hopes of becoming America's Next Top Model. We started to walk off set.

"Hang on," said the director of photography. "We have to shoot you guys leaving again. Can you walk back and get in your original positions? Back to one, everyone!"

We trudged back into line, impatient to break for lunch.

"Imagine if you had to reshoot walking out after being eliminated," said Jenah.

"Oh my god," I replied. "Like, I know you're devastated, but could you just . . . re-devastate yourself?"

We all decided to come up with a hand gesture that meant "fuck this shit" in case such a thing ever happened to one of us. It could also be used anytime we were not allowed to talk and wanted to convey that particular sentiment. We would hold our right hand high in the air and let it go limp. It was childish and silly, and I loved it.

After reshooting, we walked back to the green room, where, if our first elimination was any indication, we were going to be waiting for a long time, several hours at least. There would be a break somewhere in the middle where we'd get a meal, but otherwise we'd just be sitting in this room, not allowed to talk or leave. A handler doled out our iPods one by one. I took mine and went to find a corner to curl up in.

"Can we have our books?" Victoria asked the handler.

"No," they answered.

"Why not?" she asked, and we all perked our ears up.

"I don't have them," they answered.

"But somebody here does have them, right?" said Victoria,

which was a fair question but still shocking to hear. We all looked up from our music.

We were all occasionally snarky to the crew, resisting in subtle ways, but she was outright pushing back. She had a point, though. They'd taken the books at the same time they'd taken the iPods, so it stood to reason that they had them here. Victoria seemed completely aware of the absurdity of our situation at all times. She was always able to have some perspective, which I admired so much. Nothing seemed to shake her sense of self. In the more heightened and insane moments, she would look around at us, baffled, hoping we would catch her eye and laugh with her. I did whenever I could. She was always right: we were surrounded by absurdity. But sometimes I couldn't bear to look anyone in the eye. My reactions were too unpredictable, my sense of self too lost, and I decided it was better to retreat inward.

The judges and producers chided her for being logical and analytical and trying to use her brain to tackle the issues the show would throw at her—trying to pigeonhole her into a Smart Girl storyline, since she was studying at Yale. As though a model using her brain were a character flaw. Furthermore, they hated that she would, in moments like these, use logic against them.

They had our books, and we were going to be sitting for hours with nothing to do, not allowed to speak; therefore, they should give us our books. It seems so obvious. But it felt radical for her to speak like that to a handler.

"Can you at least explain *why* we can't have our books?" she asked.

After a while, and some more pushback from Victoria, they agreed to get them for us.

"Do not get any ideas, and do not get used to this," they told us. "You can have your books for now, but if you misbehave, we will take them back."

We grabbed at our books like they were life preservers. I ran back to my corner, so grateful to have something to quiet my running mind. I didn't want anyone to have to go home. And this week, we were all pretty sure it was going to be Kimberly. We were right.

She saw the writing on the wall too. "I have so much more to offer," she pleaded to the judges during her critiques, which were especially harsh. It was hard to watch. Kim had been a bright, sunny spot in all our days. She got along with everybody and was the mediator in all our conflicts. A few of us cried when she was eliminated.

AND THEN THERE she was again. After we were done with the elimination, they brought us to another soundstage, and when we walked in both she and Mila were there, looking at us with bittersweet expressions. What was happening? We waved to them, mystified but not allowed to talk. The camera crews weren't even there.

It turns out we were shooting the intro credits for the show. "I had to shoot our intros the day I got eliminated," Kimberly told me when I talked to her for this book. "I was gutted."

They put us in silver swimsuits and had us look down and then up to the camera, piercing it with our gaze. I hummed the theme song in my head while I did it and tried to be as fierce as possible. I couldn't imagine how Mila and Kim must feel. How do you feel fierce when a panel of judges just tore you down?

The next day, Whitney, a handler who had also been on the cruise ship, arrived to drive me to a chiropractor's office in her own car. It felt illicitly informal, like breaking the fourth wall of my whole world. As we drove, I looked around. It was my first time in LA, and up until now I hadn't been able to see any of it. The van's windows were covered, and we were always rushed inside wherever we went. It didn't look how I expected, with all its dense trees and hidden driveways.

"So, this is LA," I said.

"This is it! Well, this is a part of it. This is where the rich people live. Where we're going, you'll see some real LA."

"That makes sense. This barely even looks like a city, it's so green."

"Yeah, you know how New York has, like, suburbs outside of it?"

"I did not know that, but I'll take your word for it."

She laughed. "Okay, well, most cities have suburbs that surround them, but LA is so big that the suburbs are just part of the city."

As we continued to drive, I started to feel like I was having an out-of-body experience. I looked down at myself, sitting in the car with a woman who, although I'd been around her every day for weeks, was basically a stranger. It would be my first time at a chiropractor since I was eleven years old.

The chiropractor's office my mom had driven me to back then had a tiny lobby, and the staircase up to the treatment rooms was winding and dark with forest-green carpeting. I remember staring at my feet as they trudged up the steep stairs the afternoon of my first visit. I was nervous but excited. So far, this whole scoliosis thing was an adventure. I'd been singled out by the gym teacher who first noticed it, taken aside, and given grave, solemn attention, the best kind. I'd even gotten to miss school, dramatically walking out to my mom's car in the middle of the day on a Wednesday. The doctor had taken x-rays and was waiting to discuss them with my mom and me.

"She has moderate to severe scoliosis," he said, showing us the S curve of my spine. I liked seeing myself up on the wall there. My bones looked eerie and beautiful, all lit up in black and white, veering back and forth inside me.

"It's honestly right on the line, so we could try and treat this with a brace, or we could do adjustments and treatments in the office every week. Cost-wise, it's about the same," he said, "so it's really up to you."

I could barely stand the feeling of a turtleneck, so I was pretty sure a brace would kill me. I looked at my mom. She looked at me. She didn't even have to ask.

"We'll do the treatments."

So I started going once, sometimes twice a week. And at first, it was almost relaxing. I would arrive, and the doctor's assistant would strap me to a table that would slowly separate into two pieces underneath me, expanding and adjusting my spine. I'd lie there for longer and longer each week, and it might sound like a medieval torture device, but I kind of liked it. It felt good to be all stretched out like that, and my mind could just wander and daydream. Then the doctor would adjust my spine, carefully putting pressure on the two places where it curved until it cracked. I always left feeling taller than when I'd walked in, and I'd sing along to the radio with my mom or my stepdad on the drive home.

After a while, though, my back started to hurt, especially during soccer practice. It wasn't that bad, but I quickly realized I could milk it to get out of things, so eventually my mom took me to the doctor.

"Totally normal," my pediatrician assured us. "She's developing and also adjusting her spine, there's bound to be some growing pains. Try Tylenol, heating pads, and massaging arnica oil on the affected area."

It's true I was developing, and fast. Over the past six months, I'd grown six inches and five bra sizes. I hated it. None of my clothes fit, and I didn't like how people treated me differently now—like they wanted something from me that I didn't know how to give. Attention was my favorite thing in the world, but this attention felt . . . different. Different, terrifying, and addictive. A man followed me down the street in his car one day, and when I told my mom, she said I'd better get used to that kind of thing. *What* kind of thing? I wondered.

One day, after strapping me in, the chiropractor's hand paused on the middle of my back.

"You are looking more and more like a woman every week," he said, running his fingers up and down my spine. I held my breath and stared at the legs of the table pushing into the green carpet. He left.

My stepfather rubbed the arnica oil on my back. I was lying on my stomach, with my shirt pushed up to expose my lower and mid-back. He slid his hand up to touch the bottom of my shirt. I held my breath.

"Roll over," he whispered, barely audible.

I froze, unsure if I'd heard what I thought I'd heard. He said it again, a little louder. I rolled over. He massaged my stomach, my chest, my hips, and then my breasts.

"You've grown so much. Sometimes I wish . . ." he said, trailing off. I stared at the ceiling, not for the last time.

I stopped going to the chiropractor soon after that and completely blocked it all from my memory. And now, here in the car driving through Los Angeles, I felt like I was going to die, and I didn't understand why. My heart was beating out of my chest, and I couldn't stop swallowing. Everything sounded like I was underwater. I had to do something to remind myself that I was a human. To get back to Earth.

"What is it like working on this show?" I asked.

"Oh, man," she said. "Honestly? It's okay. The hours are crazy, but it's okay. The money's pretty good."

I felt a distant pang of anxiety. Normally, I worked all summer and saved the money to use all year, and this summer, clearly, was different. I had no idea what I would do in the fall.

"What are the other crew members like?" I asked. "Like, what are the cameramen like?"

"You know the tall, bald guy?"

"Yeah," I said, immediately picturing him in my mind. "The one who wears a lot of purple."

"Yeah. He's wild. He has a purple motorcycle."

I asked her for more details about the crew and savored every one like a tasty morsel. It was like learning that your elementary school teachers have lives outside of class. Soon we arrived at a white stone building with teal window shades and art deco details.

"This is the most 'LA' chiropractor's office I've ever seen," I said, thinking of the office I'd been to back home in Massachusetts.

"Don't get too excited; we're in a terrible neighborhood, jeez," Whitney said, looking around nervously. I looked around too, seeing only sun and bright colors.

The camera crew filmed me walking in and going back to meet the chiropractor, who took x-rays of my spine and legs. They filmed me standing, wearing the heavy lead vest to protect my insides. Then they filmed the doctor as he pinned the X-rays to the wall and went over the results for me. I hated seeing my body on the wall like that. My bones still veered back and forth.

"So, what I see here is moderate scoliosis, which you've probably had for a few years at least."

"Yeah, I got diagnosed when I was in fifth grade. They thought maybe I would have to go in a brace, but they fixed it with adjust-ments and stretching. Is that why I walk like that?"

"No," he said matter-of-factly. "A lot of models have scolio-sis," he continued. "It's common in taller women, but it doesn't usually impact your walking. I think what's making you walk like that is your hips. One of your legs is about an inch longer than the other, which isn't uncommon, but usually our hips will adjust to compensate for it. What's unusual about your anatomy is that the angle of your hips exacerbates the anatomical difference in your legs, and that's why you walk like that. Do you have hip pain or low back pain?"

"Sometimes," I said, "especially when I run."

"Yeah, running would put a lot more pressure on one hip than the other, so that makes sense."

"So, is there anything I could do?" I asked.

"Not really," he replied indifferently. "I mean, adjustments and stretching can help with the pain, but they're not going to shorten your leg, so I think that's just going to be how you walk."

I frowned and looked at the producer, unsure of what to do. This felt like the end of the road, and I didn't know where to go.

"Can we get some kind of insert for her shoe?" asked the pro-ducer. "Something that could balance out her hips?"

I perked up.

"I mean"—the chiropractor winced—"we could do a platform for her shoe, but here's the thing: an insert is only going to fix one of the issues, and it's not going to be good for her to wear it all the time."

"But maybe I could just wear it when I was on the runway," I said.

"Yeah, that could work. We could make you an insert, and if you didn't wear it too much, that could work. What size shoe are you?"

"Ten," I said, lying.

"Jeez. These are going to make you an eleven, which is huge. But I guess maybe that's normal for models."

I thought back to the Colleen Quen show. Even if the shoes hadn't been too small, there wouldn't have been any time to put the insert in.

"Okay. We're going to make a mold of your foot so you can wear the insert in your shoe."

He left, and the woman from the front desk came in with a kit and took a mold of my foot. She was chewing gum and could not stop staring directly into the camera. She never even broke her gaze to look at me or at what she was doing. When she was done, she held out her hands expectantly.

"Okay, now the other foot."

"Oh," I said, startled, "he said it was just for one foot."

"We do both," she said. "The kit is for both, so we always do both. It's . . . it's for both. Just remember to only wear it on the left side."

A FEW DAYS LATER, I stared down at my two new insoles. I had no idea which one I was supposed to wear. Why hadn't I written it down?

"Do you know which one I'm supposed to wear?" I asked the crew member who'd given them to me.

"Sorry, no."

"Can you find out? Or who can I ask?"

"Sorry, I don't know."

That was the last I heard about them. Tyra never brought my walk up again and neither did anyone else. I pushed it to the back of my brain. There was too much to deal with already. None of it made it to air.

THE NEXT DAY while I was doing my makeup in the mirror, I saw the camera guy who wore all purple.

"You know what I like?" I said to my reflection. "Purple motorcycles."

"How did you know that? Are you a witch?!" he whispered.

I grinned and walked away.

9

New Weave
Day

Bianca and I had been eagerly waiting for our makeovers, or "New Weave Day," as we called it, from day one.

"You better be ready," she told me. "It's not just black girls getting weaves anymore; they do them on white girls now too. New Weave Day could be for anyone. I bet I'm getting long, dark hair."

"You would look so good with that. Maybe like Naomi Campbell hair," I said. "I hope they make me blond; I've always wanted blond hair."

"They might give you short hair. They love your face. They always go short when someone has a good face."

"Oooh, that would be so cool."

"Really?" she asked, surprised. "I do not want them cutting all my hair off."

I'D ALWAYS WANTED to be a person who drastically changed their hair on a whim; I'd just never had the means. I love the drama of a big hair reveal: walking into a room looking like a completely different person as though it were nothing and hearing, "Oh my gosh, your *hair*!"

A few months before going on the show, I dated a vaguely attractive but very boring man. The sex was deeply unsatisfying. As boring as he was, one minor detail intrigued me. At the end of his penis was a large, round piercing. When I first saw it, I was shocked.

"Do you not like it?" he asked.

"No, no, I'm just surprised, that's all. I guess I didn't expect that you would have a piercing," I said.

"Yeah, I don't know, I just decided to do it one day."

"I get that," I said. "Sometimes I just want to cut all my hair off or dye it a crazy color or something."

"Oh God," he said, pulling a face. "If you cut your hair off, I wouldn't even want to talk to you."

Don't threaten me with a good time, I thought before leaving.

Just before I left to film the show, my new boyfriend and I laughed about the man who wouldn't talk to me if I cut my hair. It became a running inside joke.

"They might, you know," I told him. "If I go on this show, they might cut all my hair off. You'd have to put your money where your mouth is."

"I promise I will still want to talk to you if you cut your hair."

AND NOW, here I was, putting my money where my mouth was in a mansion, surrounded by the most beautiful girls I'd ever seen, desperately waiting for the show to change our hair and our lives. Every time Tyra Mail appeared, Bianca and I would hold hands and chant in a whisper, "New Weave Day, New Weave Day, New Weave Day," as a girl cracked open the card to read it. No matter what the cryptic message said, we would try to figure out a way that message could possibly be interpreted as a makeover.

"'You wanna be on top?'" read Kimberly, holding the missive that would lead us to our second photo shoot. "'It's time to learn the ropes of high fashion.'"

"We're gonna be bound with ropes or high up or something," said Saleisha.

"I'm ready to learn the ropes of a makeover," commented Bianca.

"New Weave Day will come!" I assured her.

"I have to last until at least the makeovers," said Ebony. "I can't go home before they fix my hair."

"Same," I said.

"What's the matter with your hair?" asked Ebony.

"Nothing. I just can't afford a haircut; I haven't had one in years. My hair is so long I look like I was homeschooled."

"*Stoppp*," said Ebony.

"It's true. My best friend was homeschooled, and her hair is even longer than mine, but it's, like, thick and red and perfect," I said with a pang of homesickness.

"I just want them to fix my hair. They've been making fun of this wig since the cruise," said Ebony.

"I remember," I said, thinking back to when we were roommates on the ship, a million years and miles and worlds ago. "What do you want them to do?"

"I don't even care—it's free."

THEN, FINALLY, the Tyra Mail we were waiting for arrived.

"'Like a butterfly, a true Top Model must be willing to undergo a little . . . metamorphosis,'" read Jenah, her eyes lighting up.

There was no mistaking that. New Weave Day was here. We all screamed with excitement, except for Chantal, who looked nervous and kissed her long, perfect blond hair goodbye.

The makeovers were a much-needed respite from my now constant anxiety. Here was something where I didn't have to wonder what I was supposed to do or say, I just had to show up and sit in the salon chair. I'd surrendered myself to the producers completely; I was theirs, body, mind, and hair.

A producer confirmed what we suspected when he told us to pack a hat or a scarf to wear on our heads during interviews tomorrow "just in case." We all squealed with excitement.

The next morning, we arrived at the Ken Paves Salon with our hats, scarves, and interview outfits carefully stowed away in our oversize purses. There was even more commotion and waiting around than usual because Miss J, Mr. Jay, and Tyra all had to be made up, lit, and ready. But we didn't mind, because we got to read the magazines in the salon waiting area. We'd been away from anything connected to the outside world for so long. We immediately started devouring them in contented silence. Reading a gossip rag in a fancy LA salon hit *different* from reading it in my dentist's office back home, three thousand miles away from all the celebrities sprawled across the pages.

After they got us out and into position, they told us to say hi to the Jays as they walked in and to scream when Tyra walked in behind them.

The three of them stood next to a screen that displayed our Polaroid pictures from casting. I winced a little when my photo came up. That girl had no idea how to take a good photo—who was she? As Tyra described our makeover, the picture would morph into a CGI'd picture of what was going to happen to us. One by one, we watched as our faces transformed into what Tyra, Mr. Jay, and Miss J declared Real Models. I saw my hair get blonder and shorter until it was almost a pixie cut. I gasped and squeaked with excitement. It was just like Rihanna's pixie. It looked like the haircut sported by openly gay women I'd admired from afar in college, wondering what it would be like to be them, to be with them. It looked punk. I couldn't wait to become whoever *that* person was in the new picture.

Everyone else seemed pretty excited about their makeovers, and there weren't any drastic changes planned. Until they got to Heather. They showed her long black hair turning into a spiky pixie meets mohawk hairstyle. All our heads swiveled as fast as they could to take in her reaction.

"Ahhhh!" she screamed gleefully. "I love it!"

Tyra and Mr. Jay looked like they'd swallowed their tongues.

"She looked completely flabbergasted . . . She's expecting me to completely freak out because, oh my god, this is a huge change for the autistic girl," Heather recalled with glee.

"Well . . . we're—we're not really doing that, actually," said Tyra, and then she explained that, in reality, they weren't going to change her hair at all. The moment was so uncomfortable and awkward Tyra had to rerecord most of the audio in a voiceover later. When the show aired, you'd never know they tried to punk the autistic girl with a faux-hawk.

The hairstylists took us in shifts, so some of us got right into salon chairs and some of us got more time to sit around and read magazines. It was the first time in weeks that I felt like myself: excitable, silly, and a little impulsive. I couldn't wait to go home and walk into a room looking like a totally different person and hear those magic words: "Your *hair*!"

I looked down at my long brown hair and remembered reading something about an organization called Locks of Love where you could donate your hair to be used for wigs for cancer patients if it was long and untreated enough. I went up to a hairstylist and asked, "Is my hair long enough to donate to Locks of Love?"

"Let me see," she said, grabbing my ponytail and pulling my hair out. "Yeah, I think it is. You want to do that?"

"Yes, please!"

They went and asked a producer, and it was decided. Ken Paves himself would cut my ponytail off and then mail it in. As they sat me down in the chair, the cameras surrounded me, and Ken said, "Are you ready? This is a really great thing you're doing. Someone is going to love this hair."

The feeling of being on camera was so warm and comforting until suddenly it felt slimy. Was I doing this just for airtime? I told myself that even if I wasn't on the show, eventually I would have cut all my hair off and donated it to Locks of Love. I hoped it was true.

"Are you nervous about having short hair?" asked Ken.

"No," I said. "I've actually always wanted it, but my mom has short hair, and I was afraid I'd look too much like her."

"You don't want to look like your mom?" said Ken teasingly.

"Oh, no," I said hurriedly. "I look so much like my mom, like, *exactly* like her."

"Then she must be beautiful," he said.

"She is. People always say we look like sisters, which I know is supposed to be a compliment for her, but I'm always like . . . does that mean I look old? I guess it's not that I don't want to look like *my* mom, it's that I don't want to look like *a* mom, you know? Like a soccer mom."

"I don't think you're going to look like a mom. I'll make it super edgy. I'll even dye your eyebrows. That's such a model thing."

Soon enough, I was standing up from the chair, running my hands over my new short hair and my exposed neck, feeling like a real model.

WHEN IT WAS my turn to shoot, I walked to the set and saw the wardrobe table, which looked unusual. There were no outfits, no clothes of any kind. Instead, we would all be wearing different brightly colored strips of fabric that the stylists, Masha and Anda, would be wrapping around us in elaborate knots and drapes. Mine were indigo.

"This is going to look so hot with your hair and your eyes," said Anda or possibly Masha as she wrapped fabric around my waist and threaded it through my legs.

"So hot," agreed Masha or possibly Anda, down at my feet, having just rubbed my legs with baby oil.

I felt hot. I felt tan and leggy and blond and shiny and fucking hot. I began shooting with the photographer and really went for it, jumping at every click of the camera. I lunged and really put those thin, limp strips of cloth to the test.

"Yes!" said the photographer. "More!"

"I don't want to pop a boob!"

"Girl, don't even worry about it," they said, "we can edit out a little nipple in post. Just keep the straps somewhere in the vicinity."

Almost immediately my boob popped out and I just put it back in, like I was fixing a piece of machinery. I smiled to myself, thinking how lucky I was to be in a place where my inappropriate humor and wayward tits were accepted as normal. Maybe I could find a way to be myself on the show, my old self, the preshow Sarah.

When they interviewed me about it, the producer seemed surprised at how excited I was.

"How do you feel about such a drastic change?" he asked.

"Amazing. I've always wanted short hair."

"Your hair was so long before, weren't you a little bit sad to see it all go?"

"No, honestly, I wasn't sad at all about cutting all my hair off. I've always wanted to go short! And I got to donate it to a good cause!" I hoped he'd ask more about Locks of Love and make me look altruistic.

"Are you worried it's going to look masculine? Or do you think it's fierce?"

"Honestly, I'm not worried about short hair making me look masculine at all, I think especially because I have such a curvy body. I love having an edgier look. It's so fierce."

"Are you worried that this will make you look even curvier? That maybe you'll look more plus-size?"

"Well, I hadn't been worried about looking curvier with this haircut, but I kind of am now," I said, a little defeated. I felt Show Sarah, with all her new anxieties, pouring back into me. Worried about every move she made. Bracing for moments like this. I suddenly felt tired.

"Were you nervous about wearing something so revealing at the photo shoot?"

"I wasn't nervous about wearing something revealing at the photo shoot," I answered, carefully bringing the question into my answer. "I don't know, I guess I just figured it was part of the job. I wouldn't even care about posing naked."

"But weren't you worried, as the plus-size contestant, about baring your stomach? And showing so much skin?" he asked.

"Honestly, I was more worried about my boob popping out at

the photo shoot than showing so much skin, but don't worry, it totally did," I quipped, trying to hide that I was, in fact, crestfallen. I didn't care about being naked or revealed as sexual. I cared about being revealed as fat and sad. Revealed to be an Other. Less than because I was more than. I smiled politely and wanted to throw up, or at least walk away. But I didn't get to say when the interview was done.

"Do you think your makeover is going to give you an advantage over the other girls?"

God no, I thought but did not say. *I have no advantage over the other girls. I feel like slime on the bottom of someone's shoe.*

"I don't know if my makeover will give me an advantage over the other girls, but I do think I'm lucky because . . . I really like it. It sucks when you don't like your hair, so I'm just glad I got one I liked" is what I actually said.

"So, do you think Bianca is at a disadvantage? That she'll do worse?"

I walked right into that one.

"I think Bianca is going to be fine. She's so gorgeous, and honestly, I kind of love how she looks with a shaved head. She looks like such a model."

"So would you say that Bianca is overreacting to her makeover?"

"I don't think Bianca is overreacting at all. This has been a crazy stressful day for all of us. And, I mean, I would not be okay if they shaved my head, but my mom says my head is shaped funny because I was a C-section baby, so that's a whole other story."

He chuckled, but I could tell he wasn't happy with my answer. I wondered what the right one would have been. Did he really expect me to kick Bianca when she was down? I'd been conditioned and raised to always be diplomatic and nice, and suddenly that felt like a weakness.

I walked back to the salon, pulling my clothes around myself self-consciously. When I got back to the waiting area, the vibe was off. I sat down.

"What's up?" I asked Bianca.

She looked around and then leaned in close to whisper: "Victoria found a piece of paper that, like, had a list of our names on it and then what our personalities were and how they wanted to edit us."

"Huh," I said. That didn't surprise me. Of course there would be a plan for how we would be edited and portrayed. We were the characters of this season, after all. In his interview with Oliver TwiXt, Nigel Barker repeatedly and reflexively referred to the contestants as "characters" before correcting himself: "I mean girls." So it made sense to me that somewhere, people were crafting our public-facing personas out of all the footage they had. "Do you know what it said? What did it say about you? Or about me?"

"I don't know, she didn't say," said Bianca.

Jenah walked in. "Did you hear?" we asked her.

"Yeah," she said conspiratorially. "Crazy."

"I know they're going to make me the villain," said Bianca. "I know who I am."

"Man," I said. "I have no idea who I am."

"The producers know," said Jenah, and we all nodded.

I felt like this information was washing over me without really sinking in. Like it was something I should care about, even be angry about, but I felt nothing except exhaustion.

I asked David St. John, who was a supervising producer on our cycle and did most of the interviewing, about the possibility of Victoria finding something like that.

"No," he said unequivocally. "We had a very strong policy against producers carrying paperwork like that around on set."

WHEN WE GOT back to the house, we got to make some phone calls, but not before a quick lecture.

"Some of you guys have been giving away way too much information in your phone calls," a producer told us. "No locations, no names, no details at all. You can say how you're feeling, but nothing that happened. Do not tell anyone that you had a makeover, do not tell them that you look different, nothing. Seriously. We will cut you off mid–phone call if we have to."

We did the math on how long we each had and lined up for our very vague conversations. I was secretly thrilled. My boyfriend had, right before I left, started a job at a terrifying hedge fund, where he had also signed an NDA. As a result, our phone conversations had been running on fumes and vibes. But now we had a code.

"Hello?" he said.

"This phone call is being recorded for use in television broadcast," a strict male voice intoned, as if the call were coming from the world's most fashionable prison. *Click.*

"Hey," I said.

"Hey! I miss you. How was your day?"

"It was good. You'd still want to talk to me," I said.

"Cool. It's true. I will still want to talk to you. Do you still want to talk to you?"

"What?" I said, confused by what I thought was some kind of deep, philosophical question about self-worth.

"Do you like it?"

"Yeah," I said, a hesitant smile spreading over my face. "I do. It's cool. Will you send me some rocker tees?"

"Rocker tees?"

"Yeah, like, cool rock and roll T-shirts. Because I'm not basic anymore. I'm edgy now," I said sarcastically.

I wanted to tell him that I felt like a deflated balloon after the interview at the photo shoot. That I felt further and further outside of myself every day. That I'd lost touch with all the offbeat and unabashed parts of myself that had probably been what had gotten me on the show in the first place. That I was afraid he wouldn't actually want to talk to me when I got back. Not because of my hair, but because I was too changed. That this new, on-camera version of myself was here to stay and I'd never be able to go back to who I was before. But I couldn't say any of that, even if I'd been allowed to, so I decided to focus on things I could control: my wardrobe, which I wanted to reflect my cool, edgy haircut.

A few days later I got a package in the mail, and I ran into the walk-in closet to open it away from the cameras. As I peeled the box open, I noticed that it had been opened and searched before it got to me. Inside were two bright yellow surfer-style T-shirts. I cracked up. It was a fool's errand to ask a cis straight boy to shop for me.

There was also a CD recording of his voice, which I had no way to listen to (but I did pore over the accompanying letter and liner notes he'd written for it). As it turns out, he apologized for the shirts: "I have a feeling those are not what you are looking for. I'm sorry. I can barely shop for myself, let alone for another person. When you get home, I'll buy you one—you can pick it out."

After the makeovers, we got a full day off. I spent almost all of it in the pool or in bed, lounging in one of my new T-shirts. Bianca was spending most of the day in bed too, but it was the depressed flavor of bed instead of the luxuriating one. After attempting to dye her hair blond, the hairstylist and Mr. Jay had decided it was too damaged and overprocessed, and the only thing to do was shave it off. They gave her a "medical-grade" wig to wear on shoots, but it still looked like a wig. Now, Bianca seemed so sad but also like she didn't want to be vulnerable in front of us. Most of our conversations up until now had been about New Weave Day, and it had gone so wrong for her that I didn't know what to say.

"You look better bald than most bitches do with hair," I offered nervously.

She let out a rueful laugh. "I'll get there," she said, pulling up the covers and rolling over. "I just need to get used to it."

We were all getting used to our new looks. We took turns preening in front of the mirror, looking this way and that at our new reflections. Jenah and Chantal both got long blond extensions, which they loved but were proving difficult to brush. They looked like Marcia Brady staring at their reflections while they gingerly pulled brushes through their hair, trying not to pull any of their tracks out.

"It feels so weird. It's not very edgy," said Jenah, who was anything but basic.

Lisa had gotten short hair, which she was struggling with. "I look like a poodle," she'd say, half laughing, half wailing. "Or like Bozo the Clown. This doesn't look anything like the picture on the screen. Like, what do I do with this?"

"Dude," I commiserated, "I have no idea. I thought short hair would be easier, but you can't just throw it into a bun or a ponytail. You have to, like, style it. I'm hopeless at doing my hair."

I thought back to my friend from college who had figured out that I was going on a reality show and warned me that they would probably cut my hair off. She was right, they did cut it all off. That felt like a million years ago. I looked in the mirror and tousled my hair. I didn't really care about styling it today. It was just going to get wet anyway. I went upstairs to make myself the dish I'd been eating for every lunch since I got here: fat-free re-fried black beans, low-fat shredded cheese, fat-free sour cream, adobo seasoning, and hot sauce.

"How can you eat the same thing all the time?" asked another girl.

"I don't know," I answered. "I've always been like this. I just eat the same thing for weeks."

"I do that too," said Heather.

"Me too," said Jenah. "Wait. Are you eating out of a cake pan?"

I looked down. I was, in fact, eating out of a cake pan. ". . . no?"

"You totally are. What's up, Cake Pan?" Jenah joked.

The next morning, I borrowed someone's gel, and Jenah helped me style my hair into something reasonable. Sitting on the sink counter with my feet swinging while she fiddled with bangs, I felt like a little kid staring up at her.

"You look great, Cake Pan," she said.

I got dressed in a black spaghetti strap tank top, white shorts, and ballet flats that hurt my feet. We arrived at a giant warehouse in the Fashion District filled with racks and racks of beautiful, sparkling designer clothing. Nigel was there, and he introduced his wife, Cristen Barker, a stunning, petite woman with big brown eyes. "She's a former model, a celebrity makeup artist, a mum, and my amazing wife," Nigel gushed.

I was surprised Nigel was married. Everyone on set, in interviews and during panel, seemed to be working off the assumption that we all had a crush on Nigel.

"There's Nigel, looking so hot," Tyra would say when she introduced him.

"What did you think when you saw Nigel?" the producers would ask. "Do you like British accents? Do you think the other girls have a crush on Nigel? Do you?"

At first, I played along, but it was starting to get uncomfortable to lie so blatantly. He's a good-looking man, but I didn't find him attractive at all. He wasn't my type, but also, I felt protective of the girls he really seemed to go after, Victoria and Ebony. He kept telling them to "smile more" and "be more appetizing," and it got my guard up. I also suspected that people were fooled by his accent out of noticing that he was often quite rude.

Then he introduced the CoverGirl consultant who would be judging the challenge, Brent Poer. The challenge was a timed makeup challenge. We had to put on some pink robes, do our makeup, find the dress with our name on it hanging somewhere in the warehouse, put it on, and run back and walk down the runway in front of the judges.

Afterward, as we were standing onstage and getting feedback, I was wondering how much longer we'd be there when Brent announced that I was the winner. It would have been Janet, but she put on the wrong dress. I snapped my head forward. *What?!* I giggled and wiggled all over the stage.

"You did a wonderful job," said Nigel.

"It was a big gamble to do a winged eye!" said Cristen.

"A big gamble!" agreed Brent.

"It's the only eye I know how to do," I said, still nervously fidgeting and biting my lip.

"Can I give you some advice?" asked Nigel, his voice serious, almost stern. The room got quiet.

"God, yes, please," I said, and meant it.

"You looked really wonderful and poised up there until we started to compliment you, and then you kind of . . . fell apart, and it was very off-putting. And this happens in panel as well, you seem very pleasant and confident until you get a compliment, and then you refuse to accept it. If somebody compliments you, fight that urge to deflect and fall all over yourself. Say thank you and stand up straight."

My face was burning, but I had to give it to him. That was excellent advice. I think of him every time I get a compliment now. In that moment, he started to grow on me. Maybe he wasn't rude after all. I recognized in his tone an intense desire or even compulsion to let me know the truth. It was the same tone I used when I felt misunderstood.

After the challenge was over, a crew member gathered up all the makeup—for face, eyes, and lips—from the three stations and poured it out onto a table.

"If you guys want any of that, you can have it. Otherwise, it's just going to be thrown away."

We ran toward it.

"Wait!" said another crew member.

My eyes narrowed.

The second crew member walked over with another trash bag full of makeup and poured it onto the already huge pile.

"Okay, go nuts."

We did. We all grabbed handfuls. I ended up with a trash bag full.

"How are you going to use all that makeup?" asked Victoria.

"I'm not," I said. "I'm going to bring it to my friends and let them have it."

I could just picture pouring it all out for them to enjoy. It felt good to think of the future, to think of home. Then a crew member came over and told us we could keep the dresses from the challenge.

Best day ever.

We sat around together admiring all our free new stuff and gossiping.

"There's a rumor that was going around LA that Nigel sleeps with a girl every cycle," said one girl. Our heads all swiveled in unison.

"What?!"

"Oh my god."

"Is it true?!"

"I don't know," she continued, "but I was surprised when I found out he was married."

"I was surprised too!" I said. "Why are they always asking us if we have a crush on him if he's married?!"

"Right?" agreed a few other girls. "They're always talking about how hot he is."

"I mean, he is pretty fine," said Saleisha.

"Not my type," said Lisa.

"Me neither," I agreed.

"Who do you think he likes this season?" asked one girl.

"Ebony," we all (except Ebony) said in unison.

"What?" said Ebony, pulling a skeptical face. "Why would you say that?"

"Because he loves you," answered one girl.

"He's, like, obsessed with you," said another.

"Yeah, but then he says all these terrible things too. Like, he always puts me down."

"Yeah, that's how men are," someone said, and we all nodded in agreement.

I felt great. I had good gossip and a literal trash bag full of free stuff.

Then it was time for interviews.

"So, tell us what happened today," they told me.

"We arrive at what turns out to be the Fashion District, and it's Nigel and some other people."

"Can you go back and tell us about seeing Nigel there?"

"We see Nigel . . . It was pretty great. That made my day. I was like, okay, I can go home now."

I wondered how long this uncomfortable bit would go on. I pictured the producers watching, expressionless, checking their clipboards, while Nigel and I had unenthusiastic, staged sex for the cameras.

Winning a challenge had really thrown my insecurities for a loop. Even though Brent had said Janet would have won if she hadn't grabbed the wrong dress, I decided not to focus on that. I'd been operating under the assumption that I could go home at any minute, and now, for the first time, I started to entertain the thought that maybe I would be here for a while. Hell, maybe I could win this thing.

Jesus Christ, I wrote in my journal. *Am I America's Next Top Fucking Model?! That can't be right.*

AND THEN CAME the Tyra Mail. It was my turn to read it.

"'Are you ready . . . to be deflowered?'" I said.

"We're gonna be naked," said Chantal immediately.

A chorus of agreement rippled through the group. *Fuck.* I didn't want to do a naked photo shoot. It wasn't the actual being naked I was dreading. I'd run around the house naked. I was dreading the interview that would inevitably follow.

The next morning, I looked myself up and down in the mirror. I was wearing the edgiest outfit I could find in my suitcase: a white button-down shirt with a black vest that I normally wore by itself (the early aughts were a wild time) and black jeans. My hair was unstyled, and I had no makeup on. Janet was always doing affirmations and manifestations and reading chapters of Rhonda Byrne's *The Secret* like it was the Bible: poring over the pages and whispering its wisdom to herself in moments of doubt or strife. I teased her but also envied her. If I had something reassuring to say to myself right then in the mirror, I would have, but my mind was blank. I sighed.

You look great, Cake Pan, I told myself, and headed out to face whatever the day would hold.

At first, the day held a long drive followed by an even longer wait in the van, where most of us fell asleep. And when we emerged, it was a whole other world through the van doors. We were in the mountains, surrounded by trees and next to a babbling brook. It looked like a movie set, which, I realized, it was. Or, rather, a rural location that was frequently rented out to be a movie or television set. If a tree falls in a mountain ranch resort, and there's no film crew to record it, does anybody care? We walked by elaborate wooden platforms where we'd be posing, surrounded by all kinds of fake greenery and flowers.

We walked into the hair and makeup trailer, where Mr. Jay told us that we were all going to be dressed up as different flowers and plants. The second he said "dressed" I breathed a sigh of relief.

We were all divided up among the hair, makeup, and wardrobe stations. They took Victoria and me into a trailer with Sutan, who asked us, "If I said one of you was going to be ivy and the other was cactus, which would you guess was which?"

I looked at Victoria. She shrugged. "I . . . would guess that Victoria would be ivy," I said, thinking of how thin and willowy her arms were, like ivy. "And I would be cactus," I continued, thinking of the curves of a cactus.

"Wrong, you're ivy, and Victoria is cactus."

"Cool!" I said. Sutan showed us some sketches, and we got to work transforming into our respective plants.

The makeup, hair, and wardrobe were more elaborate than ever before: airbrush, stencils, shaping our hair like plants, and using fake flowers to construct our costumes. But the crew and the photographer were fighting the light, and they kept coming in to rush the team.

"It's going to be what it's going to be," Sutan would tell the anxious crew members, not looking up from their work: painting ivy-green lines all over my face. Then Christian, the hairstylist, created '20s-style finger waves in my hair, which I was obsessed with. I kept looking at myself in the mirror, a totally different person from who I'd been that morning. The transformative power of hair and makeup still blew my mind.

I walked to the set, where they had us put our legs through a hole in the wooden platform and then covered us with the plants we were posing as, our bodies and arms "sprouting" out of the ground. Yet again, it took a little bit of trial and error, but I quickly found myself back in the zone. Mr. Jay, who was in a surprisingly chipper mood, patiently waited.

"I know you," he said. "I know you're just figuring it out. I can't see them, but I know you're modeling down to your toes. Now I just need you to bring it to your face."

The photographer, Lionel Deluy, looked like a walking Ed Hardy ad. His denim hat, vest, and torn pants starkly contrasted with his strong French accent. "Come to me, come to me, beautiful, baby, yes, yes," he said, like Pepé Le Pew with a camera. The two of them talked over each other a lot, but I mostly tuned them out.

I walked back to the holding trailer, and I could hear a girl crying before I even got through the door. I walked in, and she was sniffling, holding out a piece of her costume with a tiny red stain.

"I got my period and I stained it. I don't know what to do. This is the worst day."

A bunch of girls and I swooped in, ready.

"Okay, we got this. Cold water. Scrub, scrub, scrub, like this," I said, doing the motion my mom had taught me when I was thirteen. "Then rinse it again."

She wiped her eyes.

"Masha and Anda are not going to care, they are cool as hell, you'll be fine," said one girl.

"I was a mess during my photo shoot."

"You'll be okay," said another girl, rubbing her knee. We were all a team, a united front.

Later, during the interview, they asked me how I thought everyone else did and if anyone had gotten upset.

"Did you know that whale sharks are the biggest fish in the ocean, followed by the basking shark?"

Suddenly I didn't feel bad that I wasn't doing what they wanted; it felt right. I was having fun. I might not know the right thing to say, but I had spent my childhood planning to be a marine biologist. I had enough shark facts to last me until the finale.

At the elimination that week, Tyra made so many flower and plant puns I started to wonder if she was being sponsored by Miracle-Gro. The French photographer was a judge, and he looked confused the whole time. They kept having to ask him to say something about the photo or the girl being critiqued.

"Sorry," the director would say, "can we cut? Lionel, you haven't spoken in a while, can you just tell us what you think of Ambreal?"

"They are all very beautiful," he would say, shrugging Frenchly.

"When you get signed," he told Jenah, "and I know you are going to get signed, I am going to use you."

The other judges oohed and aahed, and I wasn't sure if they were excited for Jenah getting such high praise or if they were excited that he'd said a complete sentence.

In the end, Victoria was sent home. As soon as she was done

hugging a teary Saleisha, who was on the chopping block with her, she took off her shoes. I grinned at her. She finally got to take off those heels. Tyra looked nervous; her eyes darted backstage. The director and a few producers shifted nervously as well, looking ready to lunge at Victoria.

They think she's going to throw it, I thought, and almost laughed aloud. How absurd. Victoria wasn't angry; she was clearly relieved. She walked away with her heels in her hand. Jenah and I looked at each other and raised our limp wrists up in the air.

THE NEXT DAY, I got to film my reward for winning the challenge: a video for the CoverGirl website explaining how to use its new feature, the CoverGirl Makeup Mirror, and demonstrating how to do various looks with the products. They gave me a script the night before that I diligently memorized by copying it down by hand until I knew it by heart.

"How do you memorize lines?" asked Heather.

"Honestly, I don't know. I'm sure there are tricks and better ways to do it, but I'm just doing what I did in my high school plays and writing it all down. Once I write something down, I remember it."

The next morning, Sutan came to do my makeup, Brent Poer came to coach me, and there were two teams of camera crews: one to film me and one to film them filming me. It was all very meta. They did some lighting tests, and Brent went over what we were going to be shooting and told me the tone was "very fun, very casual, like you're talking to your best friend." I did a take and made it all the way through the lines, which I was happy about. There was a pause.

"Wow," said Brent. "That was amazing. You know you didn't have to memorize your lines? We had cue cards."

"Oh," I said, "I'm sorry."

"No, no," he said. "It was so much more natural; you were really good."

"You were so good," said Sutan, which made me blush. If Tyra was the sun of our universe, Sutan was like a neighboring star of a cooler, hipper solar system.

We did a few more takes. I didn't feel as Zen as I did during a photo shoot, but I did feel more like a member of the team. Modeling was just doing what people told you to, and this was more collaborative. It was even . . . fun. I kept waiting for the other shoe to drop.

"You should do commercials," said the producer as they were packing up. "Seriously."

"I will," I said.

I felt warm and light, and for the first time since arriving at the house, I could look forward more than an hour or a day beyond the show. The rest of the world, the rest of my life, was still out there. A world where I did commercials.

"Are you trying to lose weight?" the producer asked in my interview that night.

Ah. There was that shoe.

10

A Heap of
Garbage

When the producers and judges at panel started asking me if I was trying to lose weight, I was confused. Since arriving at the house, I'd lost only one pound according to the scale in the bathroom. I knew that because I religiously weighed myself every morning and every night and then wrote down the number in my journal, just like I had every day since I was eleven years old and went on my first diet. Every single bite I'd taken for the past eight years had been agonized over, debated, and dissected. Every day was marked as a "good day" or a "bad day" based on what I'd eaten and whether it was reflected accordingly by that number on the scale. But I was confused because . . . that was normal, right?

Everyone in my family was obsessed with their weight, men and women alike. Everyone yo-yoed and crash dieted, and every fad diet made the rounds. But "fat" was an insult reserved for women—the worst possible thing a woman could be. If a woman was fat—worse yet, if she had been thin and became fat—she had failed so fundamentally as to render all her opinions and accomplishments null and void.

People often ask me, with a conspiratorial look in their eye, if any of the other contestants on the show had an eating disorder. I get it. It would be so convenient if the size zero girls were the ones who never ate or who threw it all up when they did. I can see the disappointment in their eyes when I respond, "I don't know, I was too busy with my own."

When we picture someone with an eating disorder, we picture a dangerously thin girl, when in reality studies show people of all weights are equally impacted by disordered eating. It rarely looks like what we see on TV, so much so that I was often loath to describe myself as someone in recovery. Despite the reassurances from my therapist that, yes, I had one, I just didn't look like what I *thought* people with eating disorders were "supposed" to look like. From the bottom of my heart, I wanted to look like I had an eating disorder.

My relationship to my body was already so complicated by the time I went on the show that the producers' questions about it put me over the edge. There were just too many layers of confusion, and each one added more noise, more pressure, and more chaos inside my head.

I was too big to be a model.

I was too small to be a plus-size model.

Thinner is always better.

Why are you getting thinner?

I wasn't.

I desperately wanted to.

So, when they asked me if I was losing weight, I didn't know how to answer. I couldn't tell the truth: no, I wasn't, but I wanted to. Diet culture wants us to obsess over our weight and never talk about it. Shame thrives in secrecy.

I was so tired and distracted by the show that, if anything, I was thinking about my weight a little less, except in the moments when the producers asked me about it. Nor was I thinking about food as much. I had surrendered myself so completely that it was easy to eat whatever they gave me or the same few things every day at the house. In many ways, it was a relief. They were in charge of every aspect of my life, from my hair, to what I thought about, to *when* I ate, so it felt natural.

Every day I woke up, got mic'd, and then went to weigh myself. The camera crew would always follow me to the scale, so I'd hide the number with my foot, curling up my toes so I could peek and decide how to feel about the day. Then I would go upstairs and have breakfast: a cup of coffee with cream, egg whites, fat-free refried black beans with low-fat shredded cheese, fat-free sour cream, adobo seasoning, and hot sauce. Then, for lunch, I would usually have whatever they were serving at craft services, being sure to grab extra snacks for later. If we were at the house for lunch, I had refried beans again, sometimes with a tomato and onion sandwich on the cheapest bread possible. For dinner, I had a bag of lettuce with Hidden Valley reduced fat dressing and bacon bits and a pilfered bag of chips. Nutritious? Barely. Delicious? Only to me. It did the trick.

In the past, I'd never been one of those people who can't eat when they're stressed or depressed. I'm the opposite: I turn to food for comfort. But something about this particular cocktail of stress, sleep deprivation, and lack of structure made the thought of trying anything new or eating something I didn't like completely unbearable. When I was making my grocery list, I would literally gag at the thought of most food. So I only got foods that I knew were safe. And because I was determined to save some of the thirty-seven-dollar stipend, they had to be cheap too.

Sometime after the makeovers, the camera crew started to come running whenever I would exercise. Every time I got on the yoga mat on the balcony or swam laps in the pool, I'd hear the pitter-patter of giant boots. Soon after that, David St. John started asking about it in our interviews.

"Are you on a diet?"

"No."

"Are you eating less because you don't feel good about yourself?"

"No, I'm just stressed."

"Are you trying to be as thin as the other girls?"

"No, I'm trying to just be myself."

"Do the other girls' bodies make you feel bad about yours?"

"No, I already felt badly about it."

"Lisa said she doesn't think you belong here."

"Sometimes I don't think I belong here either."

"Would you say that you hate your body?"

"Did you know sharks have eight senses?"

I started feeling defiant. Yes, I hated my body, but I didn't want to give them the satisfaction of knowing that being there exacerbated it. I'd hated it long before I got there. That was my private pity party and they weren't invited. I was sick of the pang of guilt I got in my stomach from letting them down in every interview. I couldn't figure out what they wanted me to say even if I tried, so why bother?

This week's teach was with Benny Ninja at a gymnastics center filled with trampolines and balance beams. I was excited to see him again. He looked like an overexcited little kid with his elvish grin and his workout gear, standing on a trampoline. But his jewelry and mannerisms also reminded me that he was an icon from the New York City ballroom scene. Seeing him hold those two worlds together within himself so seamlessly was mesmerizing. I couldn't look away.

He tried to teach us to pose in midair while jumping on the

trampoline. I did okay. Not bad, not good. Ambreal excelled, posing her dancer's body into pieces of art in midair. Ebony wasn't as graceful, but she was so committed and so naturally beautiful that it didn't even matter. When she threw her long, lean six-foot-one body into the air with such abandon, arms and legs overhead, I gasped, afraid she would face-plant. But she bounced right back up, and we all laughed with her as she grinned and threw herself right back into it. Benny Ninja had to give her props for her commitment. "Ebony, you are so looooong and lovely!" he said, but on the show, the editors turned it into a Frankenbite—a line edited together from multiple lines of dialogue—making it seem like he said, "You are so lost."

Afterward, we were supposed to be sitting in silence on the trampolines as the production team packed up. I was being obediently quiet when someone shifted and I bounced a little. So I bounced . . . just a little more. And a little more. Soon we were all falling over and giggling.

"No talking," said a crew member.

"We're not!" said Lisa.

He rolled his eyes. We settled down, but it happened again a few minutes later. Eventually, a camera crew came over to film us. It was probably less work than trying to get us to shut up. We started jumping in earnest.

"Sarah!" yelled Bianca with a mischievous tone.

"What?!" I yelled back.

"What does the baby think of all this jumping?"

"Y'all!" I yelled in a thick Southern accent. "This baby gon' jump up 'n out through my mouth if I don't knock it off! It's rattling around like a jumping Jehoshaphat!"

The crew member watching over us went absolutely pale.

"What baby?" he demanded. "I'm on it!" he yelled into his earpiece, where there was presumably someone yelling back at him. "Oh," he continued, still talking to the invisible person in his ear. "I see. Okay. So, you're not pregnant?"

That last part was for me, but I didn't know it.

"Sarah!" he barked. I jumped. "You're not pregnant, right?"

"Oh!" I said, startled and still bouncing. "No. It's just a joke—"

"Yeah, yeah, okay, carry on."

"Oooooh," said Bianca, also still bouncing. "You got in trouuuuuuuble."

I pulled a guilty face and pretended to pregnant waddle off the trampoline.

The next day, they drove us to an undisclosed location and rushed us inside to avoid the paparazzi before we could see where we were. It turned out to be Iceoplex, an ice-skating rink where everything was covered in a thin layer of dust and had jazzy fonts straight out of 1986. Naturally, it was freezing, and we were dressed for an LA summer, so we shivered and looked at our breath while they had us wait in the stands for them to set up the shot.

"We are literally on ice," I whispered.

"No talking," said a crew member.

"Do you think we're going to have to ice-skate?" asked another girl.

"I do not know how to ice-skate," said Ambreal. "Gosh darn it, I thought I would do well at the challenge this week. Does anyone know how to ice-skate?!"

"Seriously, girls, if you don't keep quiet, we will keep your iPods at the next elimination."

"My fingers are blue!" said Lisa, moments before we were finally brought out onto the ice, skittering like baby penguins. There was Benny Ninja in a black tracksuit with white piping.

"Today is your ultimate challenge," he said, as two ice-skaters, a man and a woman, came out and began an elaborate routine. "You're going to be posing in the air, on the ice."

As he said that, the man lifted the woman above his head. Lisa screamed.

Then Benny introduced the people who would be judging the challenge: Lloyd Eisler, a two-time Olympic medalist who would also be teaching us the moves; Ann Shoket, the editor in chief of *Seventeen* magazine, a chic woman with kind eyes; and Dani Evans, the winner of Cycle 6. I wanted to be excited to see them, but it was so cold and they were all bundled up in sweaters and coats that I mostly just felt jealous.

They brought us off the ice and gave us matching black-and-white tracksuits to wear. Then they took us to practice the flips and lifts with Lloyd and three other male ice-skaters. I was relieved to be assigned to Lloyd, who was the tallest and burliest.

I did badly in the challenge. I'd tried to make my anger look like a high-fashion pose, and the judges said it was too subdued and not clear enough.

"Were you afraid out on the ice?" asked David St. John in the interview.

"I was terrified out on the ice. I am very tall and long and awkward, and I don't want to be dropped on my head by a very small man!" I yelled in a jokey tone.

"Were you more afraid of being dropped because you're heavier than the other girls?"

"I am not afraid of heights, but I am afraid of being dropped on my head! And if you aren't afraid of that . . . maybe you've been dropped on your head too many times!" I quipped, ignoring him. The irony was that despite how terrible the interviews made me feel, I still sort of liked them. They were an opportunity to perform, to reframe the day in my own narrative, and to joke around, and David always laughed at my jokes. Despite how he made me feel, I wanted him to like me.

YET AGAIN, I was praying I could redeem myself at the photo shoot, in which we were supposed to be "high-fashion gargoyles" on top of the Omni Hotel in downtown Los Angeles. We took the elevator up to the top floor, which was empty and under construction. There were drop cloths and exposed beams everywhere. The crew led us to some stairs up to the roof, and Ambreal, who had a fear of heights, started panicking. The stairs were exposed, and you could see not only the roof, where we were going to be posing, but the ground, some sixty floors down. Saleisha and I sprang into action and stood on either side of her, blocking the view. We held on to her shaky arms and walked her up the stairs to meet Mr. Jay.

"You got this, girl, you got this," said Janet in her warm Southern drawl.

"Plus, you get to see your favorite person," Bianca joked.

Mr. Jay didn't get along with anybody, but he had been especially hostile with Ambreal at every shoot. She was so freaked out, she could barely look up at Mr. Jay as he walked over and told us we'd be posing on a giant platform, to create the illusion that we were perched on the edge of the building. The photographer was Mike Rosenthal, who seemed just as bored as he had been at the first photo shoot. After Mr. Jay finished explaining the shoot, the director said, "Mike, can we get a shot of you giving the girls some advice for the shoot?"

"Really bring the angles in your poses," he said, with all the passion of a teenage son forced to be in his mom's TikTok.

Saleisha and I walked Ambreal back, and she finally calmed

down once she got into hair and makeup. The crew, however, remained deeply stressed. Because of the construction on the floor below the roof, they had to walk two flights to go between the hair and makeup station and the shoot, and they were hot and tired and already over it.

In the hair and makeup station, everyone was hard at work. The hairstylists slicked all my hair back underneath a giant strip of rubber before sticking a ponytail to my head. I still don't totally understand how they got it to stay, but it took two people to get it on. "You have a lot of hair under here," said Christian as he battled the flyaway strands that kept popping up from underneath the fake hair.

The makeup was dark and futuristic: dramatic black eyeliner sweeping past my eyebrows paired with glossy black lipstick. "You're like a hot monster," said my makeup artist, an intimidatingly cool woman with short hair and tattoos everywhere.

Then I was wearing a black leather strapless minidress with an orange houndstooth cape and giant Lucite heels. It was the highest fashion I'd ever felt.

"I love a cape," I told Anda and Masha before trotting up to set. I got up on the platform and waited for the feeling of Zen to come over me. But something was off. I started posing, but I could tell neither Mike nor Mr. Jay was happy.

"Can you do something more dramatic?" asked Mike Rosenthal.

I tried to jump around, but the heels were too hard to balance in, so I decided to move my arms around. I felt awkward and unsure of what to do.

"What is happening there?" said Mr. Jay.

"How about some superhero poses?" Mike said.

My brain went totally blank. What was a superhero pose, and why couldn't I do it?

Afterward I walked over to Mr. Jay, and I could tell he wasn't happy. "I don't know what happened, but there was nothing gargoyle about those poses."

The blood drained from my face.

"Oh my god," I said. "I . . . I forgot that we were supposed to be gargoyles." That's why it had felt all wrong. I'd accidentally disregarded the directions they gave us.

"You forgot?" Mr. Jay huffed.

I felt a surge of rage at him. I wanted it to be his fault somehow, but I knew it was mine. I walked away before I said something stupid. I could feel him staring at me, but I didn't look back. I walked down one flight of stairs to the floor that was under construction, away from the elevator, and hid behind a drop cloth before I started to cry in earnest. I didn't want to be eliminated, but how could they not send me home after a mistake like that?

I heard someone coming and went silent, hoping they wouldn't find me. Ambreal pulled the cloth back, and we both jumped. She had clearly come to cry too, and we laughed through our tears.

"I'm going home," I wailed.

"No, I'm going home!" she cried back.

I wiped my face off. "Well, I think I'm done crying if you want the space," I said, somewhere between a sob and a laugh.

"Thanks," she said.

I squeezed her hand and then walked away, wondering which of us was right.

As it turned out, neither. But I was so convinced that I was that, during deliberation, I wrote out notes to all the girls in my journal, along with line after line of *I WILL STAY I WILL STAY I WILL NOT GO HOME I WILL NOT GO HOME.* I scribbled away, just trying to pass the time. I figured I still had hours to go.

But then someone came in to take our journals, books, and iPods. We all looked up, confused.

"Okay, ladies, we need you all to look alive and sit up."

We were all sprawled throughout the room. We gathered ourselves, looking around expectantly. This room had always just been a place for smooth-brained waiting, and now we had to look alive?

The door opened, and in walked Tyra. My brain not only switched on; it went into hyperdrive. She looked around at all of us and smiled, sitting down.

"How can I sit down so my panties don't show?" she said in a way that was supposed to be sincere and relatable but still felt performative.

After finding their marks in the room, the crew left to film something outside of the room for a minute.

"Okay, now it's just us girls," Tyra said conspiratorially, changing her face like a car shifting gears, but she still seemed to be "on." Who was under there? Who was she performing for? Then the camera crew came through the door, and she smiled, shifted gears again, and immediately launched into her speech.

"What I'm here to talk to you about today is, um, the industry and body image. Every single person in this room, if you are to continue in this industry, will hear that you need to lose weight."

I immediately looked down at my hands. I didn't want to make eye contact with anyone, and I was afraid that the other girls would look at me because, of course, I was the exception to that rule. All I'd been hearing from the producers recently was that I was too thin. Tyra talked a little more and then brought in Dani Evans. I immediately clocked how thin she was and closed myself off from her. *Fuck her.* The thought popped into my head without my wanting it to. Then Tyra introduced an "expert on body image," Dr. Laurie Polis, a round-faced woman with a giant fake ponytail, a black pencil skirt, and red lipstick. She looked like a pinup girl posing as a doctor. When she sat down and smiled at us, I desperately wanted to put my faith in her and let her fix me. But all I could think about was her in her hotel room that morning, picking out her outfit to be on TV.

Dani shared her experience of being told to lose weight when she moved to New York after winning the show. And then Dr. Polis asked us, "Just theoretically, if you were in Dani's position, what would you do?" Everyone went around the room and answered.

"I've been trying my whole life to gain weight," said Lisa.

Fuck her too—there it was again.

"I've always struggled with my weight, but it was in the opposite direction," said Heather with tears in her eyes.

Fuck her. I tried to remember how much I loved Lisa and Heather, but rage and hatred were rushing through me, almost blurring my vision. Of course, it was myself that I was angry at, but it was too dangerous to face, so I turned it on them. *Fuck these stupid bitches. Fuck that stupid camera trained on me this entire time. Fuck Tyra,* I thought with an intensity that scared me. I didn't want to be angry at Tyra. I stayed silent, hoping in vain that maybe they would just skip me.

"What about you, Sarah?" Tyra said. This time her attention didn't feel like the sun; it felt like a spotlight catching me like I was a criminal.

"I, uh, it's . . . it's weird because I'm not just too big, I'm also too small, which is pretty fantastic, got it from both sides. I just feel wrong no matter what I do." I wished I could be as controlled and measured as Tyra was. I wished I had something to turn on, but I felt empty.

"Don't give up, if this is what you really want to do. Stick in there," said Dani.

I kept my gaze on the floor. I didn't want to hate her, but I did. Was this what I really wanted to do? A sliver of doubt was sneaking in. Then I thought of the pages I'd just written in my journal: *I WILL STAY I WILL STAY.* I thought of the easy, relaxed feeling I got on photo shoots and realized . . . damn. Modeling might really be something I wanted to do. Yes. *Yes.*

"One thing you can do is listen to the positive messages and feed them to yourself," said Dr. Polis.

What kind of expert was this, anyway? I wondered. As it turns out, she was a dermatologist.

They led us back into panel. Ambreal and I held hands, preparing to be in the bottom two. And after all that, it was Janet who went home. We were shocked. Janet was the de facto mom of the house, at the ripe old age of twenty-two. I loved her funny habit of recapping a situation in a way that made it seem like maybe it wasn't so bad and then always following it up with something so sweet and comforting.

When Saleisha was struggling with her hair:

"You just cried? Because your hair is driving you nuts and you can't do nothing with it? Listen, you're gonna figure this hair thing out, you're fierce."

When Jenah broke her tooth:

"There's a big chunk missing from your tooth 'cause you bumped it on the wall and it's concrete? You know they're not gonna let you walk around looking busted."

When the producers told me there was no time for me to make a phone call:

"You crying because you can't call home and you're missing your man? Girl, this is hard, don't feel bad."

I hated to see her go but was still glad it wasn't me.

I didn't go home, thank God. I can do better, I wrote in my journal. *I think.*

The next morning, I thought we had the day off, until Jenah started yelling for all of us to come upstairs. "I would really seriously really hurry up!" She sounded about nine years old.

And then I saw Ebony practically falling down the stairs in excitement, telling us all to get our asses upstairs. I did not feel the same way. I didn't care what was upstairs. Whatever it was just meant that we weren't really getting the day off.

So I stomped and grumbled up the stairs, and as it turns out, it was Tyson Beckford, the world's most famous male model—tall, muscular, and stunning. He was there to show us how to be a spokesperson and sell things. I looked at him and then looked around at everyone else looking at him, totally transfixed. We'd been so focused and stressed that it was nice to see them all lit up and giddy like little girls. Ebony and Jenah couldn't stop smiling. He told us to pick an item from the kitchen to try to sell as though we were in a commercial. We all leaped up and ran to the kitchen, frantically grabbing at things. In a moment of panic, I grabbed a banana.

As I sat down and looked at it, I was overcome with giggles. And the more I tried to stop, the worse it got. As the other girls went up and tried to sell their cheese grater, or Popsicle, or wineglass, I hid my face in my hands because I was still laughing, almost to the point of tears. Ebony elbowed me to stop, which just made me snort with laughter. They were all making their items so seductive, and I was holding an actual phallus. What the hell was I going to do with it? I didn't want to sell a banana. I didn't want to seduce anyone. How could I cut the tension that the other girls were building?

"What's better than a lime Popsicle?" asked Chantal as she seductively sucked and licked it.

"You ever want to get things . . . real wet?" asked Bianca, before pouring some water out of a watering can.

"Tell me that it's hot and moist and exactly what I want," Tyson told Ebony as she struggled to sell her electric teakettle.

"It's hot and moist and exactly what you want," she said back, staring at him seductively.

As I walked up to sell my banana, I decided if you couldn't beat them, join them.

"Try a banana," I said in my deepest, most alluring voice. "It's refreshing, satisfying, and it really . . . fills you up."

"Ooh," said Tyson, and then I snapped the banana completely in half.

It was a trick I'd learned from a professor who, in turn, had learned it when he was in the British army and they weren't allowed to peel bananas because it was too sexual, so they were instructed to simply crack them in the middle. I'd barely passed his class, but I'd learned all I needed. Tyson jumped as the banana cracked in two. I was pleased.

LATER THAT DAY we drove to a studio, where we met Elizabeth Santiso, who was from a nonprofit called Keep a Child Alive, which was an emergency response organization for the AIDS epidemic in Africa. Elizabeth had short hair and wore a linen tunic and a big statement necklace. She looked like all the well-meaning, liberal white women I'd grown up with in western Massachusetts. Together, she and Tyson told us we were going to be coming up with a thirty-second PSA for their campaign "I Am Africa." It had to include one fact or statistic that spoke to us, the website, and a request for donations, all with a compelling theme. They gave us booklets with all the information about the AIDS crisis and what the charity was doing, as well as some props, and sent us off to put it together in the next half an hour. I was excited to be judged for something other than my looks.

I was on a team with Saleisha and Ebony. I'd gotten to know Ebony on the cruise ship, but Saleisha had remained a mystery to me. She always seemed so focused; I hoped maybe I could absorb some of that through osmosis today.

"Okay," Saleisha said, "we need to focus." An auspicious start.

"This feels like something that really matters, you know?" I said. "It feels wrong to be talking about, like, AIDS on a reality show."

"But we are talking about it. We have to talk about it," she said without hesitation. "And if we can bring some attention to it, then that's good, right? Who cares if it's a reality show or a competition or whatever."

We got to work reading the pamphlet, which had a lot of sobering information.

"Let's write down all of the facts that speak to us in particular, because those will be easier to remember and recite," I suggested.

An idea started to come together. We would highlight the women at the center of the AIDS crisis—the mothers, daughters, and sisters disproportionately impacted by the disease.

"I'll be the mother, and, Sarah, you be the daughter because . . . you can't be the sister," said Ebony.

"Wait, why?" I said, and they chuckled patiently.

I stared at them blankly before it finally clicked.

"Right," I said. "Not a sister. I'll be the daughter."

We wrote the words "mother," "daughter," and "sister" on our chests with the yellow and red paint they gave us. I wrote out the script, and then we started to divide up the lines. I kept the compelling fact for myself to say and gave Saleisha "Keep a Child Alive believes in keeping families alive with health care, childcare, and prevention." And Ebony brought it home by encouraging people to donate a dollar a day.

"This is so good!" Saleisha told me, and I swelled with pride.

Saleisha had already won two challenges, so if she thought it was good, we must really have a shot at winning. I could picture myself at the end of the day, in my interview, recounting my success, not having to talk about my weight or my body at all. We went in to record, and I could see Elizabeth smiling and nodding while we recited our lines, which we all nailed. We did it in one take, and afterward, the three of us jumped up and down with excitement.

They gathered us all up to get notes and find out the winner, and Elizabeth said that the first team, Bianca, Lisa, and Chantal, had gotten the name of the charity wrong. I tried to hide my excitement. Then the second team had a good, simple message but lacked excitement and conviction. *Amateurs,* I thought.

"Saleisha, Ebony, and Sarah, I loved the female power; I loved the sisterhood." I caught Ebony's eye and we grinned. "But we do not do prevention," Elizabeth said, and my heart sank. I'd written that line. "We do treatment," she continued. "But it was really good. You would have been the winners, but it's so important to get the facts and the details right."

So the winners were the second group, Ambreal, Jenah, and Heather.

I was crushed. After winning a challenge because of Janet's mistake, now I was losing one because of my own. To make it even worse, I had let Saleisha and Ebony down. The three winners all got baskets of Carol's Daughter products, presented by the company's CEO, Lisa Price. Lisa then held out a bowl with all three of their names in it and announced that whichever name she picked would win a special Carol's Daughter photo shoot directed by Mary J. Blige. Heather won. Watching Ambreal's face when Heather won the photo shoot for a brand that was designed for black women added a slick layer of white guilt to the regular guilt building in my stomach. It was emblematic of the whole day. And then Saleisha and Ebony were so nice, it just made me feel worse.

"Don't worry about it," said Saleisha. "It wasn't meant to be."

That evening, in the interview, David asked me how the team worked together.

"I think the team worked really well together. I really liked working with Saleisha and Ebony; I think we all delivered our lines so well."

"Do you think there was a team leader?"

"I don't think any of us was a team leader. We were all equals, I think."

"But who came up with all the ideas?"

"We all came up with a lot of ideas, and I thought they were all pretty good."

Was he trying to make me feel bad, or was he trying to make me talk badly about Saleisha or Ebony?

"But you wrote the script?"

"I wrote the script, but only after we all came up with the idea and what we wanted to say . . ."

We went back and forth some more, and I got more and more unsure and evasive.

"Why don't you want to say that you were the team leader? Isn't that a good thing?!" he finally asked, and he seemed sincerely as confused as I was.

"Because I feel guilty!" I said, louder than I expected. "I feel bad that the line that *I* wrote got us in trouble, and I don't want to say I was the team leader because I fucked it all up!"

I sighed and sat there in silence, unsure of what to say now. I'd never been that outspoken or angry in an interview before. What a mortifying cherry on an embarrassing day. The interview never made it to air.

What did make it was when they asked me about Tyson

Beckford. It was the Nigel situation all over again, with all the emphasis on how hot he was. And, again, because I just wanted to do something right, I played along. Until I didn't.

"What was it like seeing Tyson Beckford walk in?"

"We were all pretty excited to see Tyson Beckford in our kitchen; it was a total surprise. Ebony was, like, losing her mind. She was in love with him."

"Did you think he was hot?"

"I mean, yeah, Tyson Beckford is just objectively so hot. Like, he's literally the most famous male model in the world."

"Did you fantasize about him?"

"Yeah," I said dryly. "I just had sex with him in my head and . . . now I'm done."

"Do you think he thought you were hot?"

"He did look at my boobs once," I said, which was true. "Just a little bit. He was super classy about it, but yeah, I hope he thought I was hot; he's probably gonna be a judge tomorrow."

"Can you say more about what you thought about him?"

"Ummm . . ." I was over it. I flailed around for the answer I thought would let me be done with the interview. "Mrs. Sarah Beckford. Has a nice ring, don't you think?"

"Was it nice to be around a hot man like that after spending so much time with only girls?"

"No, I don't miss men."

Somehow that last part didn't make it to air either.

The next day was the photo shoot. We arrived on set, and Mr. Jay told us that, in line with the theme of the season (environmentalism), we were all going to be representing different recyclable materials, like aluminum cans, tires, paper. I was trash bags. They had massive, elaborate sets for each of the items, all of which were thrown out after the shoot.

"So, what's your deal?" asked Sutan while giving me glowy,

simple makeup. "You don't look plus-size. We've had plus-size girls before."

"Yeah, I don't know," I said. "I'm in between sizes, apparently. I guess I could either gain weight or lose weight. But I think I'd have to lose, like, thirty or forty pounds if I wanted to be a straight-size model." I had recently learned that traditional models, size 00–4, were called "straight-size" models. Anyone bigger than that, but particularly models who were size 10–16, were called plus-size models. Sometimes I wore a 6, sometimes a 12.

"Girl, you could lose thirty pounds in a month if you had to," said Sutan.

A familiar, slippery snake whispered in my ear that, yes, yes, of course I could. I just needed the right diet and more willpower. But suddenly there was another voice, and it was coming out of my mouth.

"I don't know. I don't think I could. I don't think my body is meant to be that thin."

Later, when Christian was doing my hair, he pulled it this way and that, trying to figure out what to do with it.

"No, we are not doing this," he said, "we don't want you to look like one of these soccer moms." It was so funny to hear that phrase in his thick French accent: *sock–air mooms*.

"Oh my god," I said, "please don't make me look like a soccer mom."

"I would never," he assured me.

"I already have the body of a soccer mom. I don't want the hair too."

"Don't be a crazy girl," he said. "Enough of this. You will be cool."

I wanted to believe him, but my self-doubt was too thick to be penetrated by compliments.

"You have a great body," said one of the stylists later.

"It's true," agreed the other, her mouth full of pins. "People make a big deal about dressing people who aren't sample size, but it's not that hard."

The only word I heard was "that." It wasn't *that* hard, but it wasn't easy either. I took her praise and turned it this way and that in my mind until it was sharp enough to stab myself with.

They were dressing me as a trash bag in a big, puffy black dress and accessories made of plastic bags. I looked in the mirror and felt like I was going to a futuristic, apocalyptic prom. I went on set, and Mr. Jay seemed to be in an unusually good mood.

"You know what the theme is, right?" he asked teasingly. "You didn't forget?"

"No, I didn't forget. I got this."

"Okay, I just want to make sure we don't have a repeat of last time," he said.

"Thank you! I won't. I got this!" I said.

"Okay, girl, let's do it."

I started posing. There it was, right away. That feeling.

"There she is," said Mr. Jay. Thank God.

I jumped into the pile of trash bags on the ground and spread my arms overhead, trying to look like an old Hollywood starlet.

"Nice creativity, look at you! Okay, Sarah."

I smiled. Or did I smize?

"Although you look like a heap of garbage," he quipped. "No, I'm just kidding, I don't mean that. I just couldn't resist the sound bite." He laughed.

Normally, talking to Mr. Jay felt like shouting through an opaque, miserable fog. Sometimes there was a literal delay as I'd wait for information to penetrate. But in this moment, the mists parted just enough for him to peer out and be sincere with me.

His face even looked different, as though I were seeing him for the first time.

"That's fair," I said, still on the ground. "I am a heap of garbage. Or maybe a raccoon with all this eyeliner."

"Well, whatever you are, it's working," he said. "Seriously."

My own fog lifted, and I felt confident again for the rest of the shoot. When I got off set, I saw that a few of the girls had been watching me.

"You did not look plus-size," said Bianca.

Was it something in the air today? I couldn't escape this conversation.

"Is that a good thing?" I asked.

"I don't know," said Chantal. "Do you want to be?"

"I don't know," I answered.

Later, at the house, Chantal asked me if I was losing weight.

"Honestly? No. Or not according to the scale. I'm starting to feel like I'm going crazy, because I'm looking at the scale and it's, like, the same number, but everyone keeps asking, and I can't stop thinking about how the number is literally the same? And I know I'm in between, so I'm too big or I'm too small, and sometimes I feel like I'm just . . . wrong. Wrong about my own body, wrong about everything."

"Do you think you were trash bags because of your body type?" asked a producer in our interview that night.

"Yeah, I think I was trash bags because I'm so curvy, I had a little extra to fill the bags with, you know? It was really fun. I got to jump in giant piles of trash bags like they were leaves."

"Are you losing weight?" he asked.

"I don't know," I said, exhausted. "The scale says I've only lost, like, a pound or two, so maybe it's my hair. Which begs the question: Did my old haircut look fat?" I quipped, trying to keep my tone light but also to end the conversation.

"Are you trying to be a straight-size model?" he asked.

"I'm really not. I'm just . . . so sick of talking about it," I said, more angrily than I meant to. "Sorry."

"It's okay," he said, "that's what we're looking for."

"Oh. Well . . . I'm really sick of talking about this stupid size and weight issue, and it feels like it just keeps coming up and I don't know what to do."

The next day was elimination. When I woke up that morning, I lay motionless in bed for way too long, staring at the ceiling. I didn't think I was going home, but you never know. Mostly, I was just trying to brace myself, because I knew that once I got up, I would be up for so long. There were a lot of long days, but elimination days were the longest, the hottest, and the hardest.

"We would judge for thirteen, fourteen hours with no air-conditioning. It was hellish," said Nigel in an interview with Oliver TwiXt in 2021.

"The hours are bananas, and . . . it's not normal," a crew member admitted to me.

We never knew exactly how long the day was because we never knew what time it was, but our bodies could feel the strain of it. And not knowing only added to the stress.

Finally, I dragged myself out of bed and got mic'd, and we were on our way. Hours later, when we walked into the panel, we saw that two of the judges were wearing wigs. Miss J had been wearing one at every elimination, and every week it got a little bit bigger. This week, Nigel had clearly put on one of Miss J's old wigs. The other girls laughed, but I barely even noticed. My hypervigilant eyes had gone straight to Tyra, like always, and I could sense that something was infinitesimally different in her expression this week. Her eyes narrowed in annoyance for a split second before she composed herself and put her game face back on. I wondered whom in her life she trusted enough to be herself with. It didn't seem to be anyone on set. I pictured her with those trusted few and wondered what she was like.

"Welcome to our craaaazy judging room," she said, and then I did crack a smile, because I realized what was going on. I'd gotten a glimpse past her performative armor. She was annoyed by the wig and trying to hide it. She was used to being the one doing bits at the beginning.

Nigel was pleased as punch with himself. After she introduced him, Nigel pulled off the wig and fanned himself. "That's why I don't have hair," he said.

"Yeah, that's why," said Tyra, and I stifled a laugh. This was the most fun I'd ever had at elimination.

"It's interesting," said Twiggy when it was my turn to be judged, "because when you stand in front of me, you don't look particularly high fashion, you look quite plain, but that's actually . . . that looks like quite a good fashion photograph."

She sucked on her pen thoughtfully, to hammer home how baffling she found me. *Fuck you*, I thought. She smiled at me. I smiled back.

"Those collarbones are high fashion, though. It's that little tilt of the one shoulder," said Miss J. "That's what makes this stand out from the pack."

I love you, I thought. They winked at me and I blushed.

"Mr. Jay said it felt like you were back at this photo shoot, and I agree. I love the energy; I love the downturn of your mouth. This is well done. Very, very good," said Tyra.

I wanted to bask in the glow of this moment forever.

"You seem to have lost quite a bit of weight since the beginning of this competition," said Nigel.

I wanted to shrink into a ball and disappear forever. "A couple people have said that, but I . . . I haven't," I said truthfully. The thought of saying the number on the scale aloud, on national television, was my worst nightmare, but if it would get them off my back, I would do it.

"Have you been trying to lose weight?" asked Miss J. "Dieting? Exercising?"

"I haven't even really been trying or thinking about it, to be honest," I answered, which was as honest as I could be.

"That's when it happens," said Miss J, "when you're not thinking about it."

"Should I try to gain weight?" I asked.

No one said anything. I stared at them expectantly, waiting for an answer. Crickets. Twiggy avoided my gaze. Miss J sucked her lips. No one would look at me. It was one thing to disappoint the producers in interviews; I was starting to get used to that. This was torture. To disappoint Tyra felt like death. I couldn't stand the silence.

"I've been weighing myself, and I don't think I weigh any less than when I arrived," I said.

"Well, it seems like it," said Nigel. "Maybe your dressing has changed."

"Maybe," I answered hesitantly. "Or maybe it's my hair?"

"Okay, thanks," said Tyra after another uncomfortably long silence, and I went back to the line.

After hours of critique and deliberation, Ebony and Ambreal were in the bottom two.

"It's interesting because you girls *know* how to model. But I have to agree with Jay that this week, you girls are the weakest and have dropped way low. But the judges feel that one of you has the potential to get better. And that's Ebony," said Tyra, holding out her photograph.

Ebony didn't move. We all stared at her. Immediately the air in the room changed. Ebony took a shallow breath.

"I no longer want to be here," she told Tyra, her voice trembling.

My jaw dropped. Someone audibly gasped. We all looked around at one another. Lisa was shaking her head.

"You don't want to be here?" asked Tyra.

Ebony shook her head.

"Why not?" asked Tyra.

"Just because—" answered Ebony, her voice starting to break before she could finish the sentence. "I'm sorry," she continued, breaking down in earnest.

"It's okay," said Tyra calmly. "Tell me. Talk to me."

"Modeling I don't think is for me. I thought it was, but I miss my family, and I just . . . I want to be with them, I want to talk to them every day."

"You know what I think is not for you?" Tyra said. "I don't think it's modeling. I think it's people telling you what to do. I think it's people telling you that you're not perfect. I think that's what you can't handle. But you're going to deal with that wherever you go."

"I don't—" Ebony started to say.

"You can go," said Tyra coldly.

Ebony turned to hug us.

"No," said Tyra. "You can *go*."

Ebony jumped and walked out of the room.

"Cut!" said the director of photography. "Can someone send her back in? We weren't set up for her exit shot. Can we get her back to one? We have to film that again."

Until he said that, I'd been so focused on the people in front of me on the platform that I'd forgotten that there was a world outside of us. That the platform was part of a larger stage in a huge, warehouse-size sound studio filled with hundreds of people running around so they could broadcast this moment that had felt so intimate on national television. Suddenly I saw the whole crew frantically setting up and talking over their walkie-talkies, and in the middle of all that chaos stood a girl who just wanted to go home.

She and Ambreal stood in front of Tyra awkwardly. The director told Ebony to walk straight out this time after Tyra told her to go.

"Action!" he called.

"The most unattractive thing in the world to me is a quitter," said Tyra, "and for that, you can go."

"Thank you," said Ebony, and she practically ran out of the room. At the very edge of the stage, she raised her wrist in our secret code: *Fuck this shit.*

11

Pseudo-Vampires

When I spoke to a crew member for this book, they recalled an episode where we shot a music video. "It was, like, out in some location in downtown LA, and it started at the butt crack of dawn, and it honestly went all day until, like, one or two a.m. the next day, it was the most bonkers shoot." I nodded sagely as if I knew what they were talking about, wondering if they were mistaking another cycle for mine. Days later, I stopped in my tracks as the memory crashed into me. I was *at* that shoot, and it *was* the most bonkers shoot of my life.

Ebony had just left of her own volition, which meant Ambreal, who was meant to go home, got a second chance. She was shaken but determined. After Ebony walked offstage, Tyra hugged Ambreal and said, "There's something really beautiful about this, because this competition is about giving a chance to people that really want this." We were then sent back to holding. I was bursting at the seams, desperate to talk about what happened, but we had to be on ice, as always. After judging was over, a handler would take the eliminated girl to the house to gather her belongings, and the rest of the crew would break down the set while we all sat in the van for a few more silent hours.

By the time the camera crew filmed us in the van going home, I didn't want to talk about it anymore, I just wanted to get to bed.

"Did anyone know she was going to do that?" one girl whispered.

"Mmm," said Lisa, nodding.

"What did she say?!"

Lisa nodded at the cameraman, indicating that she didn't want to talk about it yet.

"I can't believe she did that," said Ambreal.

"I'm glad she did it," said Saleisha, "because if she would have stayed, then Am would have gone home and then it would have been another week. It would have been a waste."

"I wish she'd done it earlier," said another girl. "Then someone who wanted to be here could have stayed. She wasted all of our time."

"I don't know about that . . ." someone timidly chimed in.

We all murmured dissent or agreement. I didn't know what to think. Mostly I was just in shock that it was possible for her to make a decision like that for herself. I was so deep down the rabbit hole of this world that her conviction felt foreign to me. How had she found it within herself to do what she wanted and not what they wanted? But then I thought back to all the insults the judges had hurled at her: Nigel calling her unappetizing; Twiggy telling her she was unpleasant to be around; Mr. Jay saying she was "dull as dishwater" to his assistant while she stood within earshot. I had just assumed that was to push her, that they knew what they were doing and it would all pay off in the end. But now it just seemed cruel and deeply untrue.

We got home, drained, and a few of us still had to do our confessionals. Another girl and I went in together to save time.

"Well," she said, "Ebony just went home."

"Yeah," I said. "It was wild. She asked to go home. I thought she was going to win, to be honest."

"Oh my gosh, me too! She could have won!" said the other girl.

WHEN I WENT to bed that night it felt like the energy and dynamic in the house had been permanently altered. By morning, the events of the previous day seemed like a far-off dream. Everything was back to normal, or, rather, back to abnormal. I was back in the rabbit hole. We packed up to go to an undisclosed location that turned out to be a dance studio. They gave us full-length nude bodysuits that went to our wrists and ankles with matching jazz shoes. Looking around at all the vaguely flesh-colored mesh, I marveled that we could all look so naked and so unsexy at the same time. We looked like beige worms.

In walked Tyra in a high-cut maroon leotard over nude tights and high-heeled dance shoes. Her outfit was so flattering, the contrast between us was masterful. It was exactly what I would wear if I had to be on-screen with a bunch of wannabe models. We all screamed.

"You want top model fame?" she said in an old-timey western accent, waving her dance baton at us. "Well, fame ain't free!" she cried, slamming the heavy stick on the ground for emphasis. "And right here is where you start paying . . . in heels!" She picked up her foot and held it over her head in a full split.

We all clapped and oohed, but I couldn't help but think, *Wait. Does that make any sense?*

She went on to explain that she was going to teach us how to be sexy for a music video while still being "model sexy" and not "hoochie" like a video girl. It was an important distinction, like the difference between a high-fashion magazine and a men's magazine. Saying something looked like it was from a men's magazine was the worst insult a photo could get in panel.

I felt confident that I could be sexy. I might not like my body, but I wasn't immune to how people reacted to it. And I certainly liked the idea of being sexy from the safety and distance of high fashion. "Hoochie" invited people to be turned on by me. "Model sexy" could just stay on the screen or the page.

Tyra broke "model sexy" into four mini lessons: the sexy video walk, close-up on-camera flirting, the wall slide, and the crawl. The sexy video walk was a hell of a lot easier than a runway walk. There was a lot more movement to distract from my uneven hips. Every time my shoulder brushed Tyra's as we strutted back and forth across the room, I thought, *I JUST TOUCHED TYRA FUCKING BANKS.* Even after all these weeks, it hadn't gotten old that I got to be in her presence. We got up close to the camera pretending to be coy and cute with our imaginary boyfriend. We all got nervous during this one, because Tyra came and stood right next to us, and it was like trying to shoot hoops in front of Michael Jordan. The wall sit was where we had to be the most careful about not being a video girl.

"And us curvier girls have to be especially careful here," she told me when it was my turn to show her my sit. I would be careful all the time if it meant being in the same club with her.

"Good! Pretty! Look at how strong her thighs are!" she said, and I flushed with pleasure.

For the crawl, we put on kneepads and lunged toward a camera that backed away from us as we slid across the room on our knees over and over again. I was drenched with sweat by the end of it. We did a group cheer, and then Tyra said goodbye and went to leave.

"Cut," said the director. "Can we get a closing line before you leave, like some parting words of wisdom, and then we can film your exit again?"

"Okay," said Tyra. "Just be beautiful and use your loveliness."

The director looked like he wanted to ask her for something else, but she was gone.

WE WERE TAKEN to a small theater in the same building, where we met music video director Jessy Terrero, a short, bald man with an air of authority about him. He sat next to his tall, taciturn producer, Billy Parks, and his assistant, Lisa, a cool, petite woman with short hair. They told us we were going to audition for a part in a music video for "an international and domestic star, this artist is huge." Our challenge this week would be to choose one of the lessons that Tyra taught us and do it on the stage.

This particular challenge was terrifying, but I knew it would be useful. Once we went out into the real world, we would have to learn how to overcome the awkwardness of auditions, just like this. I didn't want to do the walk—that felt too simple—and I hadn't been very good at the coy thing; also, they weren't close up, so that didn't make sense. The slide down the wall was an option, but I didn't want to be too hoochie, so I decided to do the crawl.

When it was my turn I smiled, introduced myself, walked to the back of the stage, got down on my knees, and slid across the stage at them. I understood why they'd given us kneepads; my knees were immediately covered in painful welts, but I tried not to show it. I made eye contact with the assistant Lisa and almost started to laugh, but held it together with what I hoped was a "model sexy" expression.

After we'd all gone, they called us back in and told us that this week's photo shoot challenge was the video shoot, and we were all going to be in it. We cheered and screamed, as instructed.

Then Jessy gave us all feedback on our audition.

"I have to give a special shout out to Sarah for crawling over that rough floor," he said when it was my turn. "That was a quite the crawl."

Make it up to me with the part, I thought.

They told us they'd announce the winner of the challenge tomorrow after talking to the artist.

"Okay. We'll see you bright and early tomorrow. It's going to be a wild ride."

When he said bright and early, he meant it. We got up before dawn to drive to an empty nightclub in downtown LA. We got out of the bus and into a giant trailer. Even with all eight of us, plus the occasional crew member, it felt luxurious. Just the unobstructed windows alone were an improvement.

We waited for hours as a few girls at a time were called to get their hair or makeup done, returning with strict instructions not to mess it up. I was glad I didn't have mine done right away so I could lounge. We also took turns peering through the window to try to get a glimpse of the international and domestic star who was so huge.

We'd been there for over three hours when suddenly I saw a familiar face darting between doors. Is that . . . was that . . . Enrique Iglesias? Without thinking, I screamed.

"What?!" everyone asked.

I winced. Instant regret. I shouldn't have said anything, but it was too late now.

"Did you see who it was?" asked the PA who was watching us.

I wanted to lie but didn't think I could pull it off. "Yes," I said.

She grabbed me and led me out of the trailer into the scorching heat.

"I'm sorry!" I cried, talking as fast as I could. "I won't say anything, I swear! I'm sorry!"

She pulled me into another trailer, which was totally empty. I looked around.

"Stay here," she said, and left.

Was this my punishment? Being alone in my own trailer? I stretched out on the couch and basked in the silence. Occasionally someone would peek their head in to check on me. I'd give a thumbs-up and go back to zoning out. At one point I opened my eyes and saw the face of the woman who had brought me here looking down at me. I jumped.

"You okay?" she said.

"Yeah. Sorry. Do you need me for hair and makeup?"

"No, you can't get your hair and makeup done until after everyone else knows who it is. You fucked it up."

"I'm sorry. I swear I won't tell. I'm really good at keeping secrets. I'd tell you all the secrets I've kept, but no, I won't."

She didn't laugh. I felt bad. I hadn't wanted to make their schedule harder. The regular crew had already seemed particularly on edge today, because they were mixing with Jessy's video crew, and it didn't seem like it was going well. She hung out for a while, looking at her phone, until she got word in her headset to bring me back to set. The second we walked in, the other girls dove for me.

"Who is it?" Chantal pleaded.

"You can tell us," begged Saleisha.

"Blink in Morse code," said Bianca.

I giggled and said nothing. The PA still had a grip on my arm.

Soon after, Enrique and Jessy walked in, and we all screamed. I wanted to show them that I was still one of the good ones, so I delivered an Oscar-worthy performance in the role of Girl Surprised to See Enrique Iglesias. Enrique was so tall he had to duck. He was even taller than the girls who'd already been put into sky-high heels. He walked around the room shaking each of our hands, and I looked up at him from my flip-flops and blushed, thinking that when they asked me if I had a crush on him in the interview, I wouldn't have to play along at all. His charisma filled the room, and we were all smitten.

After he shook my hand, he walked over to Jessy by the door and said, "So I have to pick just one?"

"Yeah, but don't worry," answered Jessy, "they're all going to be in the video."

Enrique walked back over to me and said, "Is this your first music video?"

"Yes," I said, my voice quivering.

"Are you nervous?"

"Oh no," I said, "not at all. Maybe a little. Yes. Very."

He laughed, and I wanted to catapult into the space-time continuum, grab my younger self by the shoulders, shake her, and yell, *You will make Enrique Iglesias laugh someday.*

"Okay," said Jessy, "we're going to go shoot some stuff with Enrique by himself probably, and then we'll figure out what we're going to do with you." He seemed distracted.

"Whatever happens, just remember, it's Jessy's fault," said Enrique, walking out. The second he was out the door, we all fell about the place, flushed and looking at one another in disbelief.

"He is so tall," said Saleisha. "I didn't think he would be that tall."

"Oh my god, me neither!" said Lisa.

"Me neither!" I said. "I would never have guessed from his other videos that he was so tall."

"Oh my god, his other videos are so sexy, this is going to be a fun day." Saleisha giggled.

I sat down next to Heather.

"So that was who you saw before?"

"Yeah," I said.

"So hot," she said.

"So fucking hot!" I replied.

"Okay, someone get Sarah to hair and makeup *fast*," said the PA into her walkie-talkie.

Someone came and rushed me to the hair and makeup trailer. A harried and annoyed-looking woman gestured to a chair, and I sat down. This wasn't the show's beauty team; they were here for the music video.

"How fast can you finish her?" the PA asked.

"We'll go as fast as we can," said the woman, organizing her brushes.

"Can she be done in forty?"

"No."

I looked back and forth like a kid watching her divorced parents fight over drop-off time.

"Under an hour?"

"Maybe."

"Okay, under an hour, I'm going to hold you to that."

The makeup artist looked up at her. "You do that."

I pressed my lips together, looked at the ground, and didn't say anything until the PA left. "Has it been a crazy day?" I asked when the door closed. I'd lost all perspective on what a normal day was, and I couldn't wait to hear.

"It is fucking insane," she said, and told me about how the crew for the show had been fighting with Jessy's crew all day. Apparently, someone from our crew had been "screaming at *everyone* like a crazy person."

"Meanwhile, we're doing makeup for the whole cast, like twenty people, and then all of a sudden there's all these camera guys in the way and we have to do all these random *Top Model* girls," she said. "Sorry," she added, remembering who I was.

"No, that's okay," I said. "I am a random *Top Model* girl, it's true. And the camera crews are annoying."

"I don't know how you handle it, they're so in your face. Is it all the time?"

"Pretty much all the time," I said. "And when they're not in your face, we're not allowed to talk."

"What?!" she said, and suddenly I wondered if I was allowed to say that.

"Yeah," I said, "if the cameras aren't on us, we're not allowed to talk. It's called being 'on ice.' I was on ice for, like, six hours this morning."

"Jesus," she said.

My hair was big and spiky, with dramatic black eye makeup and a nude lip. Then I went to get dressed, and the new stylists put me in a mesh dress over a leather bikini and eight-inch heels. I looked in the mirror, trying to figure out what character this was, and I decided she was a punk rocker. This was the kind of outfit that belonged with my haircut.

I walked to join the other girls in the basement of the club, and we all had this dark, edgy punk look, lots of pleather, patent leather, and spikes. As we sat around, I thought back to the promo shoot, when we were dressed up in similarly extreme outfits, silently sizing one another up.

It turned out they were shooting two videos today: one with us in it, and then the exact same scenes with other people, in case they wanted to replace our shots. So, in addition to us, there was another group of girls cast in the video, along with hundreds of extras.

Jessy came in and told us the video was for a song called

"Tired of Being Sorry" and that the video took place in a gothic, vampire-esque world. He'd talked about it with "Enrique, the label, and everything, and, you know, the video is about the look, the aesthetic."

Lisa had won the challenge, but Heather would also be getting a part because she fit the theme so well. After Jessy left, the vibe was tense. Heather and Lisa were the two most divisive girls in the house. And now they both had featured roles in the video.

Bianca rolled her eyes. She had been complaining for weeks that Heather didn't even have to try and the judges loved everything she did.

"I mean, you can't deny that Heather has, like, a goth look," said one of the other girls.

"Whatever," said Bianca.

Meanwhile, it was starting to feel like the producers were trying to isolate Lisa. They would ask me about her almost every day lately and never seemed happy with my responses.

"Lisa says she's not sure if you belong here. Do you think she belongs here?"

"The first time I saw her I thought she was so hot she had to be an alien or something, so, yeah, she absolutely belongs here, she is a model. Sometimes I think I don't belong here, but I assume we all feel like that sometimes."

"The other girls are all saying they think Lisa is dramatic and annoying. Do you agree?"

"I don't think Lisa is annoying. I just think she's had a hard life and a tough childhood, and maybe they don't want to hear about that."

"Do you think she's the only one here who has had a rough childhood?"

"I mean, no, I don't think she's the only one who had a tough childhood. I don't know if any of us had, like, an *easy* childhood, but it is what it is. And, yeah, sometimes she talks about it, and it's like . . . wow, that's intense, Debbie Downer."

If they kept pushing, I would start again with the shark facts because it usually got them off my back.

And now they'd both won featured roles in the video. I looked around uncomfortably as everyone was silent. Chantal and Bianca both looked pissed. Chantal got up to walk around. I went and sat next to Heather.

"You look hot," she said.

"So fucking hot!"

The music video was shot in a few locations throughout the empty nightclub, which felt like a labyrinth. Then, when they were done shooting our various scenes in smaller rooms around the club, we were going to gather for a big group scene in the basement. But first they shot Lisa's individual scene in a long hallway; then Bianca, Saleisha, and I were in a smaller side room filled with dark pleather couches, moody lighting, and chains hanging from the ceiling. They carefully positioned the three of us on two couches, with Bianca on one, holding the chains, and Saleisha and me sitting on the other.

"Can you bring your legs up?" the director asked me. I did.

He whispered to a crew member, who came over and positioned my legs exactly the way they needed them.

"Okay, that looks great. Just remember, it's a pretty tight shot, so don't move too much."

Enrique walked in with the lead actress, who was the most glamorous woman I'd ever seen. My jaw literally fell open. She was tall—in her heels she stood almost as tall as him—with long, voluminous black hair, like Rita Hayworth's. She was wearing lingerie under a full-length leather trench coat that swung open when she walked. I didn't know if she was older than us, but she certainly seemed more mature. She made me feel like a young girl. And she was curvy, like me. I couldn't stop staring. I wanted to drink her in, absorb her essence, and maybe, I don't know, let her sit on my face. She was a total pro, focused only on the director and her choreography. She barely even looked at us, which only made her hotter.

The visual theme of the video was gothic and moody. According to the makeup artist, they were very clear to never say we were supposed to be vampires, because they didn't want to have to deal with prosthetics or special effects. So it was pseudo-vampire. Vampire adjacent. And the lead role was supposed to be this not-quite-vampire seductress who was leading Enrique through her dark, underground world to suck something other than his blood.

When they called action, she pulled him into the room, took off her coat, and walked around him while we watched in the background. They did a wide shot of them and then close-ups of all of us. It didn't feel as good as a photo shoot or as collaborative as the commercial shoot. Maybe being a video girl was not for me. I tried my best to look seductive but not hoochie. Model sexy.

Afterward they pulled me aside for an OTF interview.

"Can you describe your outfit for us?"

"It's a mesh dress over lingerie."

"Do you like it?"

"I like my outfit okay, I guess. I don't know."

"Are you uncomfortable wearing so little?"

"I mean, I am wearing very little, but I feel okay."

"Is it hard being the only plus-size girl at this shoot with so many other real models?"

They kept pressuring me to say that I hated my outfit, that I hated my body, that I was uncomfortable. And I just wouldn't. Some people play two truths and a lie; I had one truth and one lie that I desperately wanted to be true. It was true that I had barely lost any weight, and while I didn't like my body, I wasn't going to say it. I was holding on to my dignity by a thread, but goddamn it, I wasn't going to let go. When the episode aired, they showed me saying things they took completely out of context—"That makes me super uncomfortable" and "I don't like it"—and made it seem like I was talking about my outfit.

But in reality, that day I felt hot. After all, the lead actress in the video had a body like mine. I didn't know how my shoot had gone, but I still walked out of that room feeling okay. After the interview, the rest of us went to lunch (or was it dinner? It was getting dark out, but I'd lost all sense of time) while they shot Heather's featured spot.

After we were done eating, someone from the video crew led us down to the basement. It was weird being around so many cameras and equipment from a different crew. It was all the same words in a different font. The second I walked into the basement, I was hit with a wall of heat. It felt like someone was blowing a hair dryer in my face. The room was packed with at least a hundred women. I thought back to that Puerto Rican hotel and understood why they never had us all together. This was overwhelming. Pleather and leather and spikes everywhere, all on sweaty, toned LA bodies.

Heather joined us.

"Oh my god," she said as she walked into the heat.

"I know, right?" I said. "So hot."

"So fucking hot!" she agreed.

Jessy told us to dance and jump and just move as much as possible for the whole shot. And we did that shot over and over and over and over again. Then they took a break to shoot the other girls. Then they did it over and over and over again. Then they had us sit around and wait for a while. And then they did it over and over and over again. I was drenched in sweat, my lunch or dinner was jostling around, and it was miserable in my eight-inch Pleaser heels. I wasn't sure how long we'd been down there, but it felt like hours. We would lean against pillars to try to cool off and rest because there wasn't room to sit down.

I realized I hadn't seen Heather for a while. I got a little nervous and kept scanning the room. She was in a corner, slumped over on the ground. I walked over to her and bent down.

"So hot," I said.

She didn't say anything.

"So fucking hot," I said again.

Nothing.

"Are you okay?" I asked her.

She mumbled something.

"Do you need some water?"

She still didn't say anything, and suddenly I realized that something was really wrong. My brain went into crisis mode, which, thankfully, is when I am at my best. I might be totally overcome by minor inconveniences, but when things are really going wrong, I am calm and collected.

"Seriously, are you okay?" I asked, before I gently lifted her head up so I could see her face. It was gray and clammy, and her eyes weren't focusing on anything. "Okay, I'm going to take your arm and put it around me, and I'm going to lift you up, okay? We're getting out of here."

She nodded. I pulled her up, and while I walked her over to a fan, I waved to the crew members that I needed some help. I sat her down, and she slumped in the chair a little but stayed upright and took the water that one of them offered her.

"She needs help," I told them, and it finally occurred to them to get the medic, who ran over and walked her out of the room. I saw her lean on him for support for a few steps and then stumble, and then she fell to the ground. Tears sprang to my eyes, and I pushed them back down. I should have been sad and scared, but instead I was furious.

He sat her down in a chair just outside, still within sight, and her head lolled back in his hand while he got on the walkie-talkie to someone. Her face was so pale it looked almost yellow, and she was gasping and shivering.

"We need to call an ambulance," said the medic into his walkie-talkie.

Suddenly she pitched forward and vomited up the water. When he sat her back up, I saw that her mouth was foaming. She passed out and started to slide off the chair. The medic caught her and gave her more water. She immediately threw that up, and she still seemed to be in and out of consciousness. A few more medics came, and one sat down, put his hand on the back of her neck, and held her hand, while the other put an oxygen mask on her face.

"Did they call an ambulance?" I asked a crew member. He shrugged.

"Did they call an ambulance?" I asked Jessy. He shook his head ruefully. He went to say something, but I walked away before he could. I went to find one of our producers.

Normally I would never talk unprompted to a crew member who wasn't a handler, but I was filled with a newfound fire. I walked up to an executive producer who was sitting, looking at footage from the day.

"Is . . . is Heather going to the hospital?"

He looked at me for a long time before answering. "No," he said.

"She needs to go to a hospital," I said.

"She's fine. Get back to set."

"She lost consciousness twice. She was foaming at the mouth.

She could have brain damage," I insisted, shocked at the words coming out of my mouth.

"Get the *fuck* back to set!" he shouted.

I wanted to talk back, but I was too afraid. My toes were gripping my giant heels in fear. Every cell in my body was screaming at me to do what he said, to apologize. Instead, I just stood there, silent but defiant.

"Listen, little girl," he said, standing up, and through my terror and rage, I stifled a laugh. I was so much taller than him—a foot and a half at least.

For weeks, they'd been pushing and pushing us, but I'd never felt like they didn't, on some level, care about us. Even if it was just on the level of basic human decency. But as I stared at this man's face, I understood he didn't care about us at all. We were just a means to an end for him.

"This is not your call. Get the fuck back to set. Now!"

I felt a hand on my arm, pulling me. I followed it. When I walked back to where Heather was, she was standing up and talking to the other girls. He was right, she was fine. I was relieved but also still furious. But I pushed my anger aside and smiled at her. Saleisha and I even did a fake "doctor's exam" with the medic's equipment. "I have to make sure there's still a supermodel in there," said Saleisha. A handler eventually took Heather to a trailer so she could rest a little.

We kept shooting until three a.m. Back at the house, there was Tyra Mail waiting for us that said tomorrow (now today) we would meet with the judges. A producer told us to do our confessionals before we went to bed. I sat in the booth silently, staring at the camera, the backs of my eyes burning with fatigue and the last burning embers of the anger that had consumed me. I had nothing to say. I stumbled downstairs and into bed.

AT THE PANEL the next day, the guest judge was, surprise, Jessy Terrero. His voice was gravelly, and he looked as exhausted as I felt. But his feedback was still thoughtful and kind.

Saleisha and I went up for judging together, since we'd sat next to each other on set. As I walked up, my heart was in my mouth. As I watched us on the screen, I was pleasantly surprised. I put my hand over my face, shocked and delighted at the sexy, confident, mischievous girl I saw.

"Sarah, I saw, like, a wicked little sexiness inside of you," purred Tyra.

"She definitely nailed the vibe that we were going for," said Jessy.

"Sarah," said Nigel, "the camera absolutely loves you, there's no doubt about that."

This was going better than I ever thought it would. "Thank you," I said happily, wanting to wiggle but trying to take the compliment like he'd said to all those weeks ago. I stayed still and straight, trying to look confident.

"But I think perhaps you're a little nervous in your body."

My heart sank.

"And I noticed when you were watching the film just now," he continued, "you actually pulled a couple of faces watching yourself. Which shows, you know, also in the film. Because you're feeling awkward about your figure."

I wanted to correct him, to say that I wasn't uncomfortable, I was delighted. "Oh no, I—"

"I agree with Nigel," said Twiggy eagerly. "There were moments where there seemed to be a slight embarrassment. I don't know whether it was what you were wearing, or I don't know. I understand how you might have felt self-conscious, with that dress on your skin. You look quite like a ham."

She smiled at me. I smiled back, hating myself more than her.

It was only now that I felt uncomfortable and embarrassed. Of course I looked like a ham. Of course it was wrong. Of course *I* was wrong. My body felt heavy and my chest tightened.

"That's a lean cut of ham," chimed in Miss J. She was being kind and it made me want to cry. "Type of ham a lot of people want to take a bite of. But that is not the best position for the shot."

I wanted to say that was the position they'd put me in.

"In her defense," Jessy said before I could, "we told them how to sit, and they couldn't move; it was a tight shot."

"That's not an excuse," Tyra retorted. "You have to make the most out of whatever you're given on set."

"You're disappearing slightly in front of us," said Nigel, and I wished it were true. "You seem to have lost quite a bit of weight."

I'd been fighting this question for so long, and I was so tired, but in that moment, I was a pit bull with one morsel of truth in my jaws, and I just couldn't let go, even if I wanted to. Everything else was amorphous and subjective and confusing, but the one thing I could hold to was the literal number I had just seen on the scale back at the house. I had lost three pounds, most of it since they'd started asking me. Surely, on a five-foot-eleven frame, that wasn't enough to warrant all of this?

"People have said that, and I haven't been trying to, but people keep mentioning it. I just . . . don't think I have," I protested.

"We all think so," said Tyra. "You know, you have to be the size to be a plus-size model."

"Whatever size she is, you're gorgeous," said Jessy. "I loved having her on set."

The kindness made me want to cry more than the criticism, but I pushed the tears down and smiled.

"Thank you," I said, dejected, and then went to the back of the line.

Lisa, Saleisha, Bianca, and Heather got good feedback, while Ambreal, Jenah, Chantal, and I were the ones on the chopping block. I didn't think they'd send Jenah or Chantal home, so I figured it would be Ambreal or me. Since Ambreal had technically been eliminated last week, I thought maybe I'd be safe. When they brought us back to holding, I didn't write in my journal like I had last time when I thought I was going home. I just tried to go to sleep, but they called us back after just a little while.

Girl by girl was called. Jenah, Chantal, Ambreal, and I were last, just like I'd thought. And then they called Ambreal's name, and I had to hide my surprise. At that moment, I knew I was going to be eliminated. What a terrifying word. What could possibly follow an elimination? It sounded so final: surely I would evaporate and cease to exist. I tried to wrap my head around it, but I felt nothing. All the noise and chaos in my head stopped as I watched Ambreal take her photo, just as surprised as I was.

They called Jenah, and then Chantal and I were in the bottom two. As we walked forward, all I could think was that I was standing next to the girl who once said she was put on this earth to model and make babies. I had no idea what I was doing on this earth, or on this show.

I tried to pay attention to what Tyra was saying, but it was too much work holding myself together. The speech I'd heard every week washed over me.

"I only have one photo in my hand. And that photo represents the girl who is still in the running toward becoming America's

Next Top Model. And I will only call one name, and the name that I do not call must immediately return to the house, pack your belongings, and go home."

I stared ahead, trying to stay upright and in control.

"Both of you are very good models, but the judges continue to say that they feel that you're not at the top of this pack. The judges feel like you, Sarah, are kind of coasting."

I wanted to say that it didn't feel like coasting from here. That I thought middle of the pack was better than the bottom. But I had no idea what would happen if I opened my mouth, so I just looked at the floor.

"You're very, very good," she continued, "but the judges feel that your place in the industry is kind of confusing right now, because models are so, so, so skinny or they're plus-size. And you're losing weight. So you're neither. And where does that leave you? It's up to you to decide. If you're not confident in yourself, how can we be confident in your abilities?"

She went on to say that Chantal had performed so badly in the music video shoot that the judges were nervous.

Everything was getting blurrier, and I thought I might faint again when, finally, she revealed Chantal's photo.

My god, I thought, *I can't wait to sleep.*

I went to hug Chantal, and suddenly all the emotions from the last few weeks started pouring out of me and I couldn't stop them. I wasn't just crying, I was sobbing. Chantal looked at Tyra, terrified and not sure what to do.

"You're still in the running to become America's Next Top Model," Tyra told Chantal, while I tried, in vain, to collect myself. Every time I tried to stop crying, it just got worse. It devolved into full-body hiccupping, racking sobs. I couldn't help but think this beautiful moment for Chantal was marred only by me absolutely losing my shit in the background.

I tried to say thank you as Tyra hugged me, but nothing came out. She tried to reassure and comfort me.

"I know it hurts," she said, taking my face in her hands. "I know it hurts so bad."

But nothing worked. I smiled and laughed and tried desperately to play along, but I just couldn't stop sobbing. She squeezed my arm and let me go say goodbye to the girls.

"I'm such a dork!" I said, still crying and laughing at the same time.

"We'll miss you," said Chantal.

"I love you," said Heather.

"You are such a dork, Cake Pan," said Jenah.

I looked up and saw that some of them were crying too. "Can you imagine if they have to have me reshoot," I whispered. They laughed. I cried some more and walked to the end of the stage. Ready to disappear, eliminated.

12

There She Is

ut I didn't disappear. I was still there. I just couldn't stop crying. A crew member led me to a little room I'd never seen before and sat me down. They got a camera set up to interview me, and I just kept crying too hard to speak.

"I'm so sorry," I choked out. "I'm so sorry."

"It's okay, hey, it's okay," a kind woman said.

I wanted to tell them that this wasn't even about being eliminated—it wasn't about anything in particular—but I couldn't get the words out. "I'll get it together in a second, I swear. I don't know what's happening," I managed to say, hiccupping through my tears.

"Hey, we don't have to do the interview now; take all the time you need."

"Th-th-thank you. I'm sorry."

A few minutes later someone came and whispered in her ear.

"Okay, we do have to go now. Someone is going to drive you to the house."

I stood up, still crying, and followed a handler out to her car in the parking lot. I was surprised to see that it was still light out. I looked around, blinking in the sunlight. I was finally drained of all my tears. Blinking was an effort. My tongue felt glued to the roof of my mouth. Every sound took ages to reach my brain. It had been so long since I'd been in the outside world. It all looked foreign and strange, like when you visit a street where you used to live that went on changing and growing without you there. When we pulled into the driveway, I didn't even recognize the house at first.

The producer interviewed me as I was packing up, which made it hard to focus on either task.

"I didn't know you wanted this so badly," he said.

"I really wanted this, I did," I said. "But I guess it's just that weird in-between thing."

"Do you think a plus-size contestant could win?"

"I think a plus-size girl could be a top model, absolutely. I'm glad they chose me, but maybe next time someone who looks like me will win."

After a while, they asked, "Do you think you could go a little faster? The girls are waiting on you to come home."

"Yes, yes, of course," I said, trying to run. I am someone who unpacks even for a two-day trip, and I'd been in this house for weeks. My stuff was everywhere and so was my brain.

"Do you think if you could do it over again you would still lose the weight?"

"I didn't lose weight," I said, praying it was the last time I'd have to have this conversation. I went in my journal and found the notes I'd written for all the girls two eliminations ago, after the gargoyle shoot when I was convinced I was going home.

I started to copy all the notes out and put them on the girls' beds. Sarah Mail.

Finally, I had all my stuff packed up, including a full trash bag of CoverGirl makeup.

"Can you fit that in your bag?" asked a crew member.

"No, I'm sorry, it won't fit," I said. "I tried."

"Okay, can we get someone else to carry that out to the car? That won't look great in the shot."

Someone grabbed my trash bag of swag.

"Okay, time to go," they said.

"If I forget something can someone bring it to me?"

"No."

"Oh, okay. Can I just take one more lap to make sure I didn't forget anything?"

"Yes."

The cameraman winced, annoyed. I ran around, looking for forgotten items and also trying to drink in the house one last time. "Goodbye, closet. Goodbye, bed. Goodbye, pool. I think I'll miss you most of all."

I ran back upstairs and walked out the door. "Bye, house," I said, ready to go home.

AFTER WALKING OUT of the house, I got back in the handler's car.

"Are we going to the airport?" I asked. A cross-country flight sounded like a good place to take a nap.

"We are not," she said.

"Okay."

"What do you want to eat? We can get whatever you want."

"Is that because I cried like a baby?"

She laughed and didn't say no.

I couldn't think of any restaurants. I couldn't think of anything.

"McDonald's?" she asked.

I vaguely recalled such a thing.

"Taco Bell?"

Right, yes, familiar.

"Panda Express?"

"Okay," I said. "Panda Express." The words sounded like a foreign language as they came out of my mouth. I was going through the motions of being a human, but none of it felt natural. I felt like a chimpanzee trying to fake it.

A few minutes later I stared down at my sesame chicken bowl. I had a few bites, coming back into my body as I slowly chewed and swallowed. I was hungry and hadn't realized it.

"How are you feeling?" she asked.

"I . . . I have no idea," I answered truthfully. "Better, I think."

I took stock. Yes, better. Still drained and unmoored, but also light and free and oddly giddy.

"This is so strange," I said. "The house is gone."

"The house isn't gone," she said. "You just left."

"Right, yeah, sorry," I said.

We chatted a little more, and somehow the individual bathroom stalls in the house came up.

"So weird, right?" I said.

"So weird! Why are there two? And the TVs!" she agreed, laughing.

"Oh my gosh, so weird! So many channels!" I said, before immediately clapping my hand over my mouth.

"What?" she said.

"What?" I said, hoping against hope that I could get out of this somehow.

"Did you just say the TV showed so many channels?" she asked, taken aback.

I tried to think of something to say. Surely by the time the words got to my mouth I would have figured out a good lie, I thought.

"Yes," I blurted out. "The TV in the bathroom worked. Fuck it. I don't even care anymore. I'm sorry. Oh my god."

Shit.

A little while later we pulled into the parking lot of a grocery store. I don't know what I was expecting, but it wasn't this. We walked in, and the handler handed me a grocery cart and told me to get some food.

"How much?"

"Enough for a week, let's say."

"Let's say?"

I walked through the aisles in a daze. Part of me expected to see Mr. Jay around every corner telling me I had to pose with all the items in my cart. Groceries, but make it fashion. But it was just regular people. I hadn't been around anyone not connected to the show for so long. I wanted to grab them and ask, *Is this real life?!*

I couldn't figure out what to buy. I didn't know if I had to pay. All the foods that had felt safe the past few weeks sounded disgusting now.

"Is there a microwave where I'm going?" I asked the handler.

"Yes," she said.

I got microwave popcorn and nacho ingredients.

As I was checking out, a middle-aged gay man in a Hawaiian shirt said, "Okay, legs!" I looked up at him and smiled and thanked him. Was this real life?

We got back in the car, and I was starting to crave solitude like a junkie. Surely, soon I would get to be alone for the first time in weeks. It had to be close. As we drove, it was all I could think about. We arrived at a hotel, and I could taste it. She walked me into a room, and I wanted to rock back and forth from sheer anticipation, but I held it together.

"Okay," she said, and I held my breath.

This was it.

"We have to call the psychiatrist."

"What?"

"To do a quick offboarding."

"Okay," I said, crestfallen.

She handed me the phone.

"Hi, how are you feeling, Sarah?"

"I'm okay."

"Okay? Would you say you're disappointed?"

"Honestly? No. I was disappointed, but now I'm kind of relieved. I just want to be alone."

"Well, that's great to hear. You can certainly have some alone time before your roommate arrives."

"What?" I gasped, my eyes widening. "No, I . . . I can't have a roommate. I can't. I can't. I can't." I knew I sounded unhinged, in front of the shrink no less, but I couldn't help it. I knew if they would just get the fuck out of this room and leave me alone, I would be less manic.

"I'll see what I can do. Sounds like you're doing fine. Goodbye, Sarah."

I looked at the handler, desperate. Surely now she would leave.

"We have a surprise for you."

I pulled a smile from the depths of my soul and plastered it on my face. "Oh?"

She handed me her cell phone.

"Hello?"

"Hey, Sarah, it's Frank!"

I looked at the phone. I looked at her. *Who the fuck is Frank?!* I wondered. And then I remembered the sweet sound guy whom I'd laughed with a lifetime ago.

"We got your friend Frank! To make you feel better!" said the handler proudly.

"Oh gosh, thank you," I said, with a weak chuckle. "Hi, Frank. How are you?"

"Good! How are you?" he said.

"Oh, you know. I've been better. Just cried on national television."

"Yeah," he said, "I heard."

"Excellent sound guy pun there."

"Thank you," he said. We exchanged a few more pleasantries, and I choked out a whale fact for old times' sake before hanging up, shaking. Surely now, she would leave.

"Okay," she said, "I just have to go over a few more things." She started going over some details, and they all just washed over me. I couldn't absorb any of it. She handed me my cell phone and my ID, which they'd taken when I'd arrived. I looked down at them in my hands. Who was that girl in my license picture?

"Is it okay if I unpack while you talk?" I asked. I needed to do something to release all this pent-up anger I had that she was still here—still talking, still making me go through the motions of being a human. I started putting the groceries away, occasionally smiling or nodding and still absorbing nothing. She kept talking, so I started unpacking my suitcase and toiletries, giving a longing glance to the carton of cigarettes, untouched for weeks.

"And then you might get a roommate," she said, and I snapped up.

I choked back the primal scream in my chest and said, "I cannot have a roommate, I can't, I can't, I can't." Whose voice was coming out of my mouth? Who was this unstable girl?

"I mean, you might just have to deal with it," she said.

And finally, she left. I stood staring at the door. I locked the deadbolt. I walked out to the balcony, smoked a cigarette, and stretched my legs out onto the railing. I looked around as dusk settled over the city and took a deep breath. I was ready to leave being a part of an ensemble cast behind and be the main character in my own story again, in a hotel room that was a far cry from the Motel 6 my mom and I used to stay at.

I went inside and drew a bath, and as I sank down, down, down, all the way under, I tuned in to the water rushing in my ears, the inner workings of my own body and mind. *There you are,* I thought. *I missed you.*

I got out, collapsed on the bed, and slept for sixteen hours.

When I woke up the first morning, I realized that the handler had taken the room key. I was a very bougie prisoner, and, frankly, I didn't care. I would happily stay in there.

A few days later and it still hadn't gotten old. I would wake up and do exactly what I wanted for as long as I wanted, and there was no one to tell me otherwise. Occasionally I'd wonder what was next, but for the most part I was just happy to stay in my surreal present moment. I'd make coffee, have it with a cigarette on the balcony. I'd write, read, do yoga, or watch TV. The room had a little kitchen with a microwave where I would make dinner, and I'd eat it on the extra bed I wasn't sleeping in. Then I would go out for an evening cigarette before my nightly three-hour bath.

But one night, I was taking in the scenery with my evening cigarette, and I saw Kimberly Leemans waving at me. My heart stopped for a second. I don't know why I thought I was the only girl in this little purgatory station. Maybe because it felt like I was the only person in the entire world. She gestured and yelled for me to go into the hall. I did, propping the door open so I didn't get locked out.

After I hugged her, I said, "Wait, how long have you been here?"

"I'm not sure," she said. "A few weeks at least."

My jaw dropped.

"Ebony is here, so is Mila, and Janet was, but she's gone now."

"What about Victoria?" I asked.

"Oh, I don't know, I never saw her."

"Do you have a roommate?"

"Yeah, I'm with Mila, but she spends most of her time at the gym, so it's okay."

"I'm terrified of getting a roommate. I don't think I can handle it. I . . . kind of freaked out when I got eliminated," I said, embarrassed.

"Oh, girl," said Kim. "I *freaked* out. Like, I was not okay."

"Oh my god, I'm so relieved," I said. "Oh God, sorry, I didn't mean that. You know what I mean."

"No, I totally know," she said.

"Wait, there's a gym?"

"And a pool on the rooftop!" she told me. "Just be careful, because we're not really supposed to go up there, but they only check on us once a day."

We sat on the floor of the hotel hallway for a while, just catching up. It was refreshing to talk to her without any cameras present. Part of me kept waiting for someone to come yell at us to be quiet. Then we went back to our bedrooms, and I got in the bath. That was more than enough human interaction for the day.

Another day, the phone rang. I stared at it for a few rings, startled. It was the handler Whitney, telling me she'd be picking me up in an hour to go on an outing. I felt like a dog being taken for a walk, but I figured it would be good to get out of the room. I got dressed, and when she arrived, she asked me what I wanted to do.

"We can go to the beach, we can go to a movie, or we could go shopping."

"I could do the beach! I'll grab my swimsuit."

"Oh, you can't really swim in the ocean, just so you know. It's too cold."

"Oh, okay, I'll go shopping. Are there any good thrift stores in LA?"

She laughed. "Um, yeah. There are, like, the best thrift stores in the world. Let's go."

It was the best shopping I'd ever done. I got a bunch of clothes to match my new, cool hair. It was the closest I've ever come to a trying-on-clothes movie montage.

I'D BEEN IN the hotel room for well over a week, and I was starting to regret that shopping spree because I was running out of food and money. The hotel had room service, but it was expensive, and the only food we could get for free, for some reason, were the chocolate chip cookies. They were delicious, but they were also getting old. I wondered if I could go grocery shopping again soon and if I could afford it.

I'm not the only one who ran out of food. When Lisa D'Amato was kept in a hotel after her elimination on Cycle 5, her handler "was sneaking food for me, like granola bars. Which is the reason why in the next episode, after I got eliminated, where Bre [Scullark] thought that someone stole her granola bars, it was because that PA went in and stole her granola bars, thinking it was production's, but it was hers."

I hate granola bars, so I was relieved when the handler called and told me I was going to be brought back to set to be a decoy—I'd get lunch on set and steal some snacks for later. The paparazzi had started to recognize the *Top Model* environmental party bus and would often be waiting for us when we came out. To throw them off the scent of the winner, they'd have eliminated girls walk in to be on set, just off camera. That's why Mila was at the

Colleen Quen fashion show. And now it was my turn. We arrived at a runway show, and they dressed me up and had me walk at the end, after the rest of the girls who were still competing. I stood across the stage from them. I couldn't stop staring at them. I was surprised I didn't miss them more. A week ago, I would have killed to be with them, but now I just wanted to get back to my hotel room. Just as soon as I stole some food from craft services.

Suddenly I realized Chantal was gesturing and mouthing something at me.

"The TV!" she hissed, and I turned bright red. *Fuck.* "Why did you tell them?!" she asked. "We got in so much trouble, they took our iPods!"

I played dumb. I didn't know how to explain that, in reality, I *was* dumb, and I'd tattled on them by accident. I walked down the runway, stuffed my bag full of snacks and drinks, and went back to my little cave.

A few days later, I ran into Ebony in the hallway. "Girl! I am going crazy! I want to go home!" she said as she ran by like an apparition.

"I kind of like it," I yelled after her. I think I was the only one who did, maybe because I didn't have a roommate.

"When I tell you that I was carving fucking notches in the wall for how long we were there," Kim recalled. "I remember doing my exit psych eval, and then it was on the phone call in the hotel. She's like, 'How are you doing?' And I'm like, 'I'm not well. I am not okay. My whole fucking world is crumbled.' I was so upset. And she was just like, 'Okay, bye.' And I was like, 'Oh.' And then I was in a hotel room in fucking isolation for two months. It was insane."

But all I wanted was isolation. And I got it for two weeks. And then the handler came to my room and told me I would be getting a roommate.

I started to panic.

"I know," she said, "but it's only for one night. You're flying home tomorrow."

"Oh," I said.

"I thought you'd be happy about that," she said, confused.

"No, I . . . I am." I didn't know how to explain to her why I wasn't. I barely knew how to explain it to myself. But the fact was, this was a tiny oasis where I didn't have to think about the future or all the unknowns in my life. I wasn't even sure what "home" I was returning to. My mom's apartment? She'd moved right before I'd left, so it wasn't exactly a homey, familiar place. I had no idea what I was going to do when I got there, and I had no money to do it with. "Who's my roommate?"

"You know I can't tell you that."

A few hours later, Ambreal walked through the door.

"Oh no!" I cried. "I'm so sorry!"

"Girl, it's fine," she said. "It was my time; I wasn't even supposed to be there. I'm so fine. I'm excited to go home."

AND HOME WE WENT. I landed in Boston! Logan! International! Airport! I walked to baggage claim and there was Michael. I thought I'd cry when I saw him, but I felt calm, relieved. My life was still here. And then came the moment I'd been waiting for all these long weeks.

"Oh my gosh, your hair!" he said.

"I know!" I said, beaming.

And I went "home" to my mom's new post-divorce apartment and tried to make a plan. I still had months before the show aired, so I still wasn't allowed to tell anyone where I'd been. I was horrified to find out that both my mom and my dad had told everyone they knew that I was on the show. I begged them to

stop and tried to instill the fear of God in them like the producers and lawyers had done to me.

"Seriously, they will sue you," I said.

"Sorry, lambie," said my mom. "You got it!"

"I just want to talk to my friend who works for the local paper
so he knows he'll get an interview with you," said my dad.

"Dad!" I cried. "No press! Seriously! Do not talk to him about
this!"

"Fine! I won't," he said. I was suspicious.

"Did you already talk to him?"

"I did."

I was so stressed about trying to get him to stop telling people
that I gave myself hives. Then, a few days later, I got a voicemail
from a producer telling me to "rein in my damn dad," and "get my
shit in order." Which should have stressed me out even more, but
somehow, as I listened to the message, I felt like a spell had been
broken. Once, this person had controlled when I could go to the
bathroom, when I could speak, how much and how often I ate,
and now it was just a tiny little yell coming out of my crappy
Nokia phone speaker. I knew that, of course, they could still exert
a lot of power over me, but it all seemed so small and silly and
distant. When he called back and we spoke on the phone, I told
them that my dad was an adult, and they could deal with him; I'd
done my best and washed my hands of the situation.

Besides, I had bigger fish to fry. I was completely out of money
and had only a few weeks before school started. I got my old job
back at the blueberry farm, but I couldn't even afford gas to drive
there on my first day. So, yet again, I found myself scrounging for
change in my mom's car and couch. I finally got enough for an
eighth of a tank, which I pumped at the same gas station where
I'd scrambled to buy cigarettes at the beginning of summer. I
stood in the parking lot. After all that, I couldn't believe I was in

the literal same place. I put my car in gear and drove up to the blueberry farm.

"Your hair!" they all exclaimed, beaming.

"Yeah," I said bashfully.

"Why'd you cut it?" asked my old boss.

"Just . . . wanted a change," I said. I hated lying to them, especially after all the things I'd said about working at the farm in my audition. I knew there was no way they'd ever find out, and, really, what did it matter? But my insides still felt slimy.

"Where have you been all summer?"

"Just traveling," I said. "I went to California."

They believed me. I hated it. I went to fix the sorting machine. After all, I was the only one with arms long enough to reach.

At least I had Maggie, my best friend from high school, who knew the truth. She was one of the people who'd signed her life rights away so I could call her, which I never did. I asked her to tell the rest of our friend group, to save me the conversation. Then we all got together at our friend Julie's house one beautiful New England summer evening. I walked up and poured out the trash bag of makeup onto the picnic table, and they all grabbed whatever they wanted.

They had a million questions about the show, and I didn't know how to answer them.

"What was it like?" asked Julie.

How do I sum up the most insane thing that's ever happened to me? How do I explain something that I don't understand?

"So surreal," I said, and told a few silly stories but avoided the bulk of it.

They all told me about their summers and colleges and boyfriends. It was exactly like I'd pictured. I might have had no idea what was about to happen, but if this evening was any indication, maybe things would be okay.

I DECIDED NOT to go back to school in Boston, to be closer to New York City. I wanted to try my hand at modeling, but I wasn't ready to drop out yet, so I transferred to a school in New Jersey where I had a few close friends, including Maggie.

I called Michael and Meredith to tell them. They were disappointed but not surprised.

In September, I headed to my new school, Drew University. The day before I arrived, they released our names and photos to the press. I was in *People* with the caption: "Is THIS plus size?" The magazine had polled readers, and apparently 93 percent of people agreed I was not plus-size. I stared at my picture on the page. How many people had they asked about my body?

My first weekend at my new school, a girl at a party asked me if I'd heard that there was an *America's Next Top Model* contestant who had just started at the school.

"That's crazy," I said.

The first episode aired September 19, Maggie's birthday. I watched with her and a few new friends, feeling bad for stealing her thunder. There was a viewing party at a coffee shop in my hometown. I covered my eyes every time I was on-screen. I did that every week. A few episodes in they showed me saying that Lisa was a Debbie Downer. I called her immediately.

"I'm so sorry," I said.

"You're good," she said. "I know how it was. They twist stuff around."

"Can I be really honest with you?" I asked.

"Um, I guess," she said nervously.

"They did twist it, but . . . I also said it, and I can't blame them. I think I was jealous of you, and not even for how you look. I mean, that too, but I was just jealous of how open and honest you were, and I felt like I didn't know how to do that. I'm really sorry."

"Okay," she said. "We're good."

"Thank you," I said.

I hung up. I wished I could be with the other girls when each episode aired. I hated watching with people who couldn't know what it was really like. I resented them for only being able to see what the producers and editors presented to them. My friends would look back and forth between the television and me, waiting for my reactions to the compressed, edited version of what I'd been through. And I looked back at them, peeking from behind my hands, desperate to see what they were seeing, what I looked like to people who didn't know the whole story.

I was relieved to see that, in the episodes leading up to my elimination, very little of their interrogating me about my weight made it to air. I'd managed to sidestep their questioning and didn't give them enough to work with. All in all, I was pretty happy with how I came across.

"You seem nice," my dad told me. "You're always helping people or doing something kind. I'm proud of you."

"You seem cool," said Maggie. "Like someone I'd be best friends with."

I smiled, but I was nervous about what would happen when she saw my final episode. I'd known Maggie for almost ten years, and she'd never seen me cry like I did when I got eliminated. The week I thought it would air, they released a bonus footage episode instead. I was so relieved; I didn't even cover my eyes when I saw myself on-screen that week.

Then I got a call saying that they wanted to fly me to LA for my elimination episode so I could do some press. I couldn't wait. It sounded so . . . famous. I packed all the clothes I'd bought in

LA and headed to the Newark airport at four in the morning. Such was the life of an Inter! National! Supermodel!

At the airport, while I was going through security, a TSA agent around my age quietly said, "Hey, I know you."

"You do? Do you go to Drew?" I asked.

"No," she said, confused. "You're from *Top Model*, right?"

"Oh!" I said. "Yes!"

It was my first time being recognized, and I hadn't even understood it. I vowed to do better next time. (Reader, in all the years since, I have never done better.)

When I hopped off the plane at LAX with a dream and my cardigan, it felt eerily familiar. A handler came and picked me up and drove me to a hotel. But this time it was just me. The solitude and quiet made me nervous. She gave me an itinerary for the next day and told me she'd be picking me up around five a.m. for a morning show interview.

Before the interview, I met someone from the PR team who would be supervising me all day.

"Be honest, be yourself, don't worry too much about it," she told me before I went in for my first-ever live interview. The host introduced me and then asked me about the video shoot and Heather getting sick. A cloud came over my face.

"They pushed us really hard in that shoot. Normally they were really good about making sure we ate, but she went all day without food and she was really sick. I was really afraid she was going to have brain damage. But she was okay; she's fine now. It was a long time ago, I don't know."

"Okay, maybe not so much about the behind-the-scenes stuff," said the PR person afterward. "And remember, for the viewers, this all just happened. It wasn't months ago; this is right now."

"Got it," I said. "Television magic."

"And remember to stress what an amazing opportunity this was."

The next interview was for PIX11 News. The host was a blond man who came alive on camera like somebody flipped a switch. Off camera, he was a completely different person.

"Action," called the director.

The host's face transformed into his on-camera mask. "Today we have recent *Top Model* eliminee Sarah Hartshorne. How are you?" he asked in a tone that let me know he was about to ask about my crying.

"I'm good, I'm great," I said in my most upbeat voice.

"Yeah?" he said. "That was . . . pretty moving at the end there."

"Yeah, it was, it was. It was a tough couple minutes, but I got through it. I'm okay now."

I tried to keep a light, jokey tone to show that I really meant it. In a later interview, someone asked me what my plans were for after the show, if I planned to keep modeling. My mind went blank, and it must have showed on my face, because the PR rep stepped in.

"Sarah is the first *Top Model* contestant in history to have booked a cover shoot before even being eliminated."

"I am?!" I asked, surprised.

"That's right," the PR person continued. "She's going to be shooting the cover of *Supermodels Unlimited* next week."

I swelled with pride. I had no idea! Inter! National! Super-model! I started playing the part.

"I don't know what the future will hold for me, but I am going to keep modeling," I said, demure but determined. I tried to channel Lisa. "Starting with this shoot, I suppose!"

I got back to the hotel and collapsed. It was late, and I had to be up and packed early the next day. I looked at my phone for the first time in hours. The elimination episode had aired on the East

Coast, and I had twenty missed calls and dozens of texts. I put my phone down. I wasn't ready to face it without having seen the episode myself.

I turned on the hotel room TV and saw they'd taken a totally out-of-context quote and made it seem like I was uncomfortable with the outfit I'd worn in the video shoot. After they'd tried so hard to get me to say it and I'd worked so hard not to, it didn't matter. They found a clip of me saying, "It made me super uncomfortable," about something else and put it over the footage of me on set. I was almost mad. But mostly I was just resigned.

Then they showed the music video, which looked amazing and was only ever shown that one time. It's nearly impossible to find online, even. The version with the other cast was shown on MTV and all the other channels, while our version is (mostly) lost to history.

I watched myself at panel and saw they didn't include the moment when I asked them if I should gain weight. *Figures,* I thought. I watched them deliberate.

"You can't just say you're a plus-size model and then not be," said Nigel.

YOU TOLD ME TO SAY THAT, I thought-screamed at the TV.

I watched us file back in and watched Tyra call name after name. I watched myself and Chantal walk forward. I turned off the TV and picked up my phone.

"*SARAH! I AM SO SORRY! THIS SUCKS SO HARD!*"

"Yo, fuck Tyra!"

"Girl, are you okay?!"

Television magic had fooled all my friends too. I didn't answer any of them. What could I say? That, despite having cried four months ago, I was fine now? That I'd been through something that I didn't understand, so how could they possibly try to?

Then I saw an AIM notification from Saleisha.

"Hey girl."

"OMG hey," I said, so relieved to talk to someone who understood.

"Heard about the cover, congrats!"

"Thank you!!!!"

We caught up a little bit. It turns out she never got to go to Paris and model in Colleen Quen's show.

"How's ur hair?" I typed. "Did u get to change it back?"

"Yeah, I changed it like right away when we got back but I actually have that same hairstyle again now," she said.

My stomach lurched like I'd driven over a hill too fast. I immediately put the puzzle pieces together. She'd hated that hair so much; I could think of only one reason that she would have it again: she was the winner. I wasn't surprised or mad. I just felt . . . left out. They'd all gone on to have more adventures without me. I didn't even know where she'd gotten back from.

THE NEXT MORNING, I had a few more morning radio show interviews before my flight. The PR person gave me some pointers for how to do radio: keep it short and sweet, avoid gray areas. She told me that there would be more interviews when I got back, mostly morning radio shows like these.

"We'll send you some guidelines on how to handle them, but it's mostly just talking on the phone! You're good at this!"

"Aw," I said, "I bet you say that to all the girls."

"I do, yeah," she said.

The now defunct *Supermodels Unlimited* was a magazine for pageant girls and aspiring models and a place for scam modeling schools to run ads. Its pages were filled with heavily photoshopped faces that looked like very sexy dolls. But I didn't know any of that when I showed up to the salon in New Jersey where the shoot was taking place. I was just happy to be there.

The creative director and hairstylist, Eric Alt, a tall gay man who owned the salon, started pushing my hair this way and that before starting.

"How do you like this blond?" he asked.

"It's okay. I don't know. I can't really afford to maintain it."

"Yeah, your roots are really long. We can touch it up, but it would be faster to go dark. How would you feel about that?"

"Oh my gosh, yes. Let's do it!"

"Makeover!" he said.

As he was blowing it dry, I looked at myself in the mirror, excited that my last two haircuts and colorings had been free. Which was good, because almost all the money I'd made on the blueberry farm was already gone. I usually worked all summer, but now I had only a few weeks' worth of savings.

"Will you take us out for drinks after your fancy magazine shoot?" a new friend of mine at Drew had asked.

"Oh, it's not paid," I said, and he looked more disappointed than I was. "Sorry."

But it was still fun as hell. They gave me a dramatic smoky eye and a nude lip. Very high fashion. Then the stylist put me in a voluminous black chiffon shift and red high heels with matching gloves. It was avant-garde, and I loved it.

The set was dark and moody, so I matched my face to it. I did the broken doll move and swung my head back and forth, my face aloof.

"Yes," said Eric. "Girl, you can *model,* look at you! Let's go even weirder!"

He had his assistant use lighting equipment to create shadows that went back and forth over half my face and body. It was like he was painting with shadows.

We shot until late in the night and squealed over the shots when he uploaded them. I was so happy with them.

Supermodels Unlimited, however, was not. They never ran them. They also never called to set up the interview. The whole feature was scrapped.

I GOT A job tutoring students and another one taking care of an elderly invalid woman in her home. I worked thirty to forty hours a week and then had classes on top of that and was still waking up at five most mornings to do interviews. I did so many interviews that these canned responses became my new version of the truth. I didn't know how to process anything that had happened; it was much easier to wrap my head around the PR version.

One week, I had six dollars in my bank account and I lost my dining card. Until the replacement card arrived in the mail, I was living off what I could get from a broken vending machine in the basement of my dorm that spit out two snacks or sodas every time.

"So, Sarah," asked a morning radio show host, "what are you having for breakfast today?"

This wasn't one of the stock questions I'd gotten used to answering, so I told the whole truth.

"A Diet Dr Pepper and some Goldfish."

"Oh my god, that is such a model breakfast," crowed her cohost.

"Actually, it's all I can afford," I said.

There was an uncomfortable pause. They changed the subject. I snapped back into the answers I knew they wanted to hear.

I was working too much to watch most of the remaining episodes, but the moments I did see were conflicting. On the one hand, it was the only time I got to see the girls again, whom I desperately missed. On the other hand, it felt like looking at pictures of a party I'd been kicked out of. In the episode after I got eliminated, Heather said she missed me, which made my heart pang. And they all went to China, which made me jealous at first.

"Dude, China suuuucked," said Jenah one late night on the phone. "We were all covered in welts from mosquito bites."

And, as it turns out, some of the decoys from the hotel went to China with them. They still weren't allowed to leave their rooms. "I felt so bad for them," said one crew member who was there. "They were literally locked in their hotel room with a production assistant, staff member, what have you, looking after them, but they weren't even allowed to have the key to their room; they had to stay in their room. It's almost like they were prisoners." One of the decoys was Ebony. After she asked to leave the show because she missed her family, they kept her locked in hotel rooms for almost two months.

"We brought Ebony. She wanted to leave the competition, and then we were like . . . sorry, no, you can't go home, which was torture to her," said David St. John, when I interviewed him for the book.

I loved my time in the hotel (although who knows how I would have felt after two months). I'm such an introvert, I needed that kind of time and space to reconnect with myself. I was relieved to see that I wasn't the only one feeling that kind of disconnect during shooting.

"I feel like I'm losing myself. I just want to know who I am in this competition, and I want to know who the judges think I am," said Jenah, a few episodes after I was eliminated.

"The hardest part about this competition is that everything that I feel, like, made me strong is just . . . flown out the window," admitted Lisa in another.

I felt an ache I didn't know what to do with. I watched the

show and wished that I could be with them in China instead of in New Jersey, spending my days helping kids write essays and wiping an old woman's ass while her husband watched. But they'd left China months ago. The TV magic was working on me too.

On December 13, 2007, the final episode aired.

Well, the whole damn thing is over and done with, I wrote in my journal. *Saleisha is America's Next Top Model, but I already knew that. It's a meaningful, educational experience that culminates in . . . what? And is it a meaningful experience? Educational, maybe, but meaningful? It's on my mind all the time, but I still hold firm that it doesn't define me. Whatever.*

13

Was It Terrible?

After my elimination episode aired, I was free to try my hand at a modeling career. To prepare, I'd made a list of New York City agencies that represented plus-size models, and the second I was legally allowed, I started to submit applications and go to open calls. I met Nolé Marin, a former *ANTM* judge who owned an agency, at a fashion show competition we were both judging, and he agreed to meet with me.

I went to his office in midtown Manhattan and sat on a plush leopard-print chair. He sat down opposite me, hands in his lap, lips pursed, looking me up and down.

"I mean, first things first, you need to lose about thirty pounds," he told me.

I stared at his round frame. "Oh, no, sorry, I know—I want to be a plus-size model," I said.

"Oh," he said, confused. "I mean, have you thought about just losing thirty pounds?"

I smiled and shrugged. I thought about what the dermatologist had said and tried to feed myself some positive thoughts.

"My agency doesn't do plus-size girls, but I can put in a good word at Wilhelmina if you want. They have the best curve board around."

"That would be great!" I said excitedly, filing away the knowledge that "curve" was another word for "plus-size."

"But I should warn you," he said, "nobody is going to sign a plus-size model with short hair."

He was right. I met with agent after agent, and they all said some version of the same thing: "Come back when your hair is longer." Including Wilhelmina. None of them said I was too thin. None of them seemed to care much about *Top Model* either, except as an explanation for why my hair was too short. One agent put it this way: "We want fat, happy girls with fat, happy teeth and hair." I thought back to all the women in my mom's Newport News catalogs.

So I kept working, saved up my money, and got my teeth whitened. And then my boyfriend gifted me hair extensions. I dropped out of school and moved in with him to save money and to really give modeling a shot. I got a job working at a chiropractors' office with a flexible enough schedule for me to go to photo shoots and castings.

I was terrified to tell my grandfather that I was leaving school, but he surprised me.

"This is a bizarre opportunity you've stumbled into," he said.

"Yeah, and I want to make the most of it," I said eagerly.

"Well, I think that's wise, I do," he reassured me. "School will always be there for you. And modeling certainly won't be there forever."

"I don't want to do this forever," I said.

"And you can't. There will be an expiration date. Just remember that."

The extensions were terrible and didn't match my real hair,

but they worked. I signed with a boutique agency called IPM Model Management. My agent was a stunning retired plus-size model who spoke with an even-keeled, husky purr and then composed all her emails in caps lock.

I thought that signing with an agency meant the money would start pouring in, but as it turns out, I still had to pay for test shoots to pad my portfolio. If you couldn't afford test shoots, sometimes agencies would loan you the money and deduct it out of your checks. I decided not to do that and just tried to work with cheap or even free photographers, much to the chagrin of my agent: "Girl, *there are only* two or three good shots. Why not just spend the money on a good photographer?!" But good photographers charged around $500.

Eventually, I cobbled together enough photos to fill my portfolio (which agencies also charge for, deducting sixty to eighty dollars out of your first check). Back then, it was a physical book with your agency's name on the cover. I loved carrying it, under my arm, all around the city to castings and ever so casually handing it over to clients. Inside were photo prints (another sixty to eighty dollars) and comp cards, which are like oversize business cards for models; they have your measurements, your headshot, and your agent's info on them.

"Should I put my *ANTM* photos in my book?"

"Maybe in the back," said my new agent. "You can't really tell what you look like under all that makeup and foofaraw."

Agents and clients might not have cared much about *Top Model*, but it seemed like everyone else did. My burlesque troupe manager was right: it did change how people saw me. I watched people start to treat me differently when they found out. Whether it was better or worse, I still hated them for it and kept a running tally of anyone who acted that way.

In some circles, I was ashamed to admit that I'd been on the show. This was in the early days of reality TV, before reality stars and influencers became the "new aristocracy" that the TV critic George W. S. Trow predicted in his anti-television essay "Within the Context of No Context." Back then it was novel to meet someone from the Wild West of unscripted content, but I knew that some people would take me less seriously because of it, so I preemptively developed a self-deprecating tone when it came up.

"I was on *America's Next Top Model*," I'd say. "I did not win. I was America's Next Seventh from the Top Model."

And I still used the same canned answers to the questions people pressed me with for details.

"What was it like?" they'd ask.

"Surreal," I'd say, and leave it at that.

It was true, but like canned fruit, it lacked any of the peach fuzz or seeds. There was no nutrition or potential for growth. Whatever didn't fit into a funny story was discarded. When I talked about ripping the tiny medical gown at my preshow physical, I never stopped to think about the fact that I didn't know if the people who drew my blood in that hotel room were doctors; it had never occurred to me to ask.

When I first signed with IPM, I was living in Connecticut with my boyfriend and commuting into the city for castings and jobs. Jenah had moved home to Connecticut, and Victoria was back at Yale in New Haven, so the three of us hung out sometimes. We would go to big, loud parties, and we always ended up sitting together in a circle, chain-smoking and sipping from our Solo cups, not saying much. The three of us didn't have a lot in common besides the show, but it had become a presence in our lives that no one else—not our families, classmates, or partners—could understand.

"Hey, after shooting wrapped, were you like . . . so fucking broke?" I asked them, sitting around a bonfire, after taking a drag of my cigarette and setting it down on my can of Michelob Light. It felt scandalous to say it out loud.

"So fucking broke!" said Jenah. "I couldn't afford to fix those hair extensions they gave me during the makeover when they started falling out. It was awful."

"I could barely afford my books this semester," said Victoria.

We all paused.

"So fucking weird," said Jenah.

"So fucking weird," we all agreed.

Sometimes when I was in the city, I would hang out with Kimberly Leemans, who was hustling to make it as a model and to capitalize as much as possible on her time on the show. Every time I hung out with her, I felt like I got a lesson in things I should be doing. She hooked me up with invites to events, red carpets, and benefits. It felt like she knew everyone and was doing everything.

"Hey," she said one day, "come to New Jersey with me to walk the runway in a benefit for breast cancer. They're sending a limo for us."

"Who is us?" I asked.

It turned out to be three contestants from Cycle 10: Claire Unabia; Marvita Washington, whom we'd met in our cycle but had been cut in the first episode and had gone on to compete in Cycle 10; and Whitney Thompson, the plus-size contestant who had won. We walked in the show and drank and partied all night. I felt like a real model.

A few weeks later, I ran into Whitney at a casting, and we struck up a conversation. I looked down at her comp card and noticed we had the same measurements. I wondered what kinds of questions the producers had asked her about her weight. Why had her body been right and mine so wrong if we were the same size?

She and I became friends for a while. We bonded over the experience of being a plus-size model but not a plus-size person and all the mental minefields therein. She'd won a contract with Elite Model Management . . . which didn't have a curve board, so they had no idea what to do with her. Eventually, she moved out of NYC to start a restaurant. Jenah and Kim both moved to LA. Victoria graduated and left. I watched on social media as the girls I once competed with got married, had babies, went back to school, and pursued other careers. It was bittersweet watching them leave. I felt like they were giving up. Giving up what? I couldn't say.

I kept modeling, assuming I would either age out or get successful enough to do what I really wanted to do. I wasn't sure exactly what that was; I just knew it wasn't modeling. And I was starting to feel like I'd stayed at a party too long. The host was starting to clean up, but I didn't have a ride home.

I signed with a European agency and a bigger, more established one in New York. I had a few clients who booked me repeatedly, including one in Germany who flew me out once a month to shoot their catalogs. When people asked me what I did, I felt like an impostor when I answered "model," but it was the truth. After years of modeling being the side hustle, I was making a living at it.

One day I was sitting on an uncomfortable Lucite chair in my agency's lobby, waiting for my agent to call me, perusing the magazines and catalogs full of my coworkers' faces, when I noticed the woman I was waiting with was incredibly glamorous. I was pretty sure she was my age, but there was something about her that was Grown Up. She reached for her Dolce & Gabbana sunglasses with her sleek nude manicure and pushed them up on her head so her shiny, bouncy hair framed her face.

We introduced ourselves and started chatting about various castings and clients we had in common.

"Are you modeling full-time?" she asked. This was kind of a loaded question. It was a question asked to ascertain what your success level was. Most models have to supplement with other jobs, at least for the slow part of the year when jobs are few and far between. It was only a select few who could do it full-time, and I had only just broken through. The chiropractors I'd worked for had become like family and were just as excited as I was when I was able to quit.

"Yeah," I said, "how about you?"

"For now," she said, "but you know how it goes."

"Yeah," I commiserated. "We'll see what happens once I age out."

"What do you mean?" she asked.

"I mean, once I get too old to model."

"When do you think that will happen?" she asked carefully.

"I'm not sure," I said recklessly. "In my thirties, I guess."

She laughed kindly. "Honey," she said with a patient smile, "I'm forty-seven. You've got some time."

My jaw dropped, and I immediately had two thoughts strike my heart. First: *I need to get her skincare regimen.* Second: *I am not going to age out of this job.* It never occurred to me that I could get stuck modeling. I'd always told myself that everyone wanted to be a model, but, upon reflection, not even I wanted it anymore. The other girls hadn't given up; they'd moved on, and it was time for me to do the same. After all, who was I doing it for? The men in suits who had drilled into me that a million girls would kill for this opportunity?

A year later, I emailed my agencies that I would be quitting on my next birthday. To celebrate, I dyed my hair blue and got some tattoos. My American agents were sweet and understanding and wished me the best of luck. My German agency had a different response:

BLUE⸮⸮⸮
⸮⸮⸮⸮⸮⸮⸮⸮⸮⸮⸮⸮⸮⸮⸮⸮⸮⸮⸮⸮⸮⸮

(I still have the email, and she did include that many question marks.)

AFTER ALL THAT, I still didn't really talk honestly or openly about the show. I kept my canned responses on the shelf for years, always there when I needed them.

Lots of people saw the writing on the wall before I did. As time went on, more and more people would ask me, "Was it terrible? I heard it's terrible," and I would parrot, "No, of course it wasn't terrible—it was a great opportunity. I would never have pursued modeling without it. A million girls would kill to be on *Top Model*."

After I stopped modeling, I took various jobs writing and producing videos. My boyfriend—the one who promised he'd still talk to me if they cut all my hair off, who is now my husband—and I moved to New York City. The first month we lived in our tiny Hell's Kitchen apartment, I cried with happiness every day. I'd wanted to live there since I was five years old and would visit my aunt, uncle, and baby cousin who lived in Brooklyn.

Now that I was living in the city, I threw myself into stand-up comedy wherever and whenever I could. I had to write a few jokes about *Top Model*, because whenever other comedians found out about the show, that was how they'd introduce me as they brought me onstage. But it was hard to get more than a quip or two, no matter how much I tried. To really joke about it, to write about it, I'd have to examine it more than I was ready to do at the time.

Which isn't to say I didn't want to talk about it. As years went by, questions slowed but never stopped. "I'm sorry, you probably get this all the time," people would say before asking me about it. "You're probably sick of talking about it." But the truth is I never got sick of it. And maybe that's just because I am incredibly self-centered. But it also felt like I was turning it over and over in my mind every time I talked about it, like an oyster turning an irritating piece of sand over and over until it became rounded and bearable and beautiful: a pearl.

As early as 2006, there was controversy about conditions on set. The writers of the show went on strike, demanding the same benefits and wages as scripted television writers. I hadn't even known there were writers for the show—I never encountered them. Then, in 2008, Tyra came under fire for the working conditions on her daytime talk show, *The Tyra Banks Show*. A lot of my friends hoped I'd have some juicy gossip, but I wasn't ready.

"Was Tyra a nightmare to work with?" they asked eagerly.

"No. Definitely not. It was hard sometimes, but Tyra and the other producers on *ANTM* weren't malicious," I insisted, clouded by my self-imposed veil of optimism. "They were just trying to make good television."

I couldn't dig deeper until I got on TikTok. I'd been working as a producer and stand-up comedian, touring the country doing live shows, and in the summer of 2020, it had all come to a screeching halt as I quarantined with my husband in our NYC basement apartment.

How many of us discovered that cursed app in a quarantined fever dream? How many hours have we spent swiping through, letting the algorithm discover our innermost selves? No app knows us better.

"It only shows me underage girls dancing," complain my straight male friends.

"TikTok only shows you what you want to see, pervert," I reply. Which is why my feed is full of lesbians baking bread, hot trans men cooking, and the radical left-wing, BIPOC, LGBTQAI, communist agenda. It's Fox News's absolute nightmare and my very favorite thing.

I started making videos as a way to kill time in the height of quarantine and quickly discovered an audience for stories about *Top Model*. My first video about it got hundreds of thousands of views, so, buoyed by the dopamine rush, I made more. At first, finding things to talk about was difficult, like pulling buckets from a murky well. But the more I thought about it, the more I remembered.

Over the coming months and years, I built a small community on TikTok. There will always be trolls, but for the most part, I was so touched by all the support and love I got when I shared my stories.

I was surprised to find that not only was *ANTM* still relevant and interesting to people, but it was also going through a reckoning as Gen Z came to terms with the impact the show had on them as young viewers. The comments on my videos painted a new picture: "Gosh watching the way the judges talk to contestants about their looks makes me so uncomfortable," "This made me sad," "That show is sick," "Producers are so wretched on those shows." TikTok viewers were starting to pry my unwilling eyes open to the truth.

Jenah, always one step ahead of me, opened them the rest of the way. We'd kept in sporadic touch over the years, and I

FaceTimed her one day to catch up. When she picked up, I smiled at her on my phone screen, blithely chipper and optimistic.

"I'm thinking about writing a book about *Top Model*."

After some back-and-forth, eventually she let me know that this was a bittersweet conversation for her, because, frankly, she was still traumatized by her time on the show.

"I think the whole industry needs to be taken down," she said.

I told her I'd think about what she said and we'd talk more later. I hung up, taken aback. Had we been on the same show? Did things get worse after I was eliminated? Or had I just gotten lucky and somehow snuck through the reality television gauntlet unscathed?

Then I started writing. I read my own words and was shocked.

For years I'd been glossing over the details of my own memories, even in conversations with my closest friends. Stories poured out of me onto the page, stories that I'd never said out loud, because some part of me knew that if I did, they would become real. To do so would force me to see them for what they were: deeply impactful and even, yes, traumatic.

Trauma and the NDA kept everything buried down deep, although after all these years, I had a hard time being afraid of the men in suits on the cruise ship. Their words were still embedded in my brain, but they felt more like a dream than a threat. I was more afraid of facing my own memories. In many ways, I was absolutely one of the lucky ones. But I didn't make it out unscathed. I was not the first to faint, nor was I the last to realize that maybe a production where a young, unpaid girl is at risk of losing consciousness every episode needs to be examined.

And examining something that once brought us joy can be painful. *Top Model* brought a lot of people a lot of joy, both audiences and participants. And that is beautiful and undeniably good. It also harmed a lot of people. It caused equally undeniable pain and trauma. Acknowledging one truth does not negate the other. Both can (and do) exist at the same time.

The producers *were* trying to make good television. At any cost. And by refusing to acknowledge for so many years that there was any ill intent, even if the tactics they used "to make good television" were the same ones used by cult leaders to inspire obedience, I could avoid facing the truth. They took our phones and watches, and they prohibited newspapers, televisions, clocks, or anything that told us what day or time it was. They removed all of our agency and kept us on edge by withholding food, sleep, and access to bathrooms. It pains me to say it, but it would be impossible for the producers, including Tyra, not to see the damage they were doing.

Tyra Banks set out to change the fashion industry, and she did it. It is more inclusive and diverse because of her and her show. Maybe it's naïve of me, but I don't think she set out to do harm. I think she set out to create a show that opened a window into the fashion world to audiences at home, where she could mentor models into successful careers. But the show quickly outgrew those noble intentions, set aflame by toxic fuel. The very first winner, Adrianne Curry, never received her contract with Revlon. And the subtleties of the fashion and modeling world didn't translate to television, so they had to create higher and higher stakes. And in my case, those stakes did not reflect the reality of what it was like to be a plus-size model. After all the criticism, no one in the real fashion world ever thought I was too small.

The fact is the reality television industry and the fashion industry are deeply toxic, harmful industries where old, rich men take young, beautiful women and treat them like they are disposable. *Top Model* was at the nexus of both, and contestants bore the brunt of the damage. So how do we go about changing that?

Paying talent for their time and labor feels like an obvious and easy place to start. Reality shows are cheaper to make than scripted television because of exploitation. Or as Emily Nussbaum says in her seminal book *Cue the Sun! The Invention of Reality TV,* they're "the slimy beneficiaries of anti-labor tactics, funded by executives who didn't want to pay writers and actors." As someone on the receiving end of those slimy tactics, I can assure you being paid would have helped. Exploitation really hits different when you're also not being paid for it.

I was lucky enough to have resources after the show that helped me not only pursue modeling but also receive proper mental health care. That made all the difference in the world. Everyone deserves the same.

Since I began to speak critically and honestly about the show, another question has entered the rotation that I'm frequently asked:

"What would you say to Tyra now?"

It's a complicated question. On the one hand, she provided me with one of the biggest opportunities of my life. I owe her a lot, I know that.

On the other hand, I lost myself on that show. They broke me down and took advantage of my trauma. It took years of hard work and therapy to find myself again. The biggest thing I had to learn was how to see the world through my own eyes, instead of constantly focusing on how the world viewed me. To climb down from my disassociated tower where the only thing that mattered was what I looked like. Shout out to my therapist, Lisa, for giving me the tools I needed. And shout out to myself for using them.

"I think that *Top Model* is probably the biggest thing a lot of girls had ever done and will ever do," said David St. John when I interviewed him for this book. And maybe that's partially true. I mean, here I am writing about it all these years later.

But while I may not have done anything "bigger" by his metric, I know I have done better things. I had a child. She alone is better than anything in the world, let alone a reality show. I found my voice onstage doing stand-up in front of audiences all over the country. I talk about what it's like to be a retired plus-size model, a current plus-size person, a queer person, a new mom. Offstage, I found my voice by becoming part of an amazing community of friends, a ragtag group of queer weirdos from all over the world, that accepts and embraces all those things about me. A community in the city I love that, along with motherhood, has shown me who I am in ways that constantly surprise me.

For a long time, especially after I stopped modeling, I threw myself into being a Productive and Helpful Person. I defined myself by what I brought to the table. But I saw a whole new side of myself when I was forced to acknowledge what I take from the table. What I need. As a new mom, I was open and exposed in a million ways, not least of all because I simply didn't have the bandwidth to be helpful to anyone but this new, fragile, perfect life. And then, when my daughter was eight months old, I had surgery and couldn't even do that. I needed help just to nurse her; I couldn't pick her up. People warned me that the only way to survive motherhood is to ask for help, but I thought I would be the exception. I wasn't.

It was a humbling, vulnerable experience to come to the table with nothing and walk away fed and supported. An incredible honor that the old, wounded parts of me said I didn't deserve. I saw myself stripped down, unable to be pretty or sexy or helpful or even funny, which were all the things that I thought made up who I was. And not only did my friends and family still love me, but I loved myself. I used every tool my therapist and I had come up with over the years. It was hard and unsteady, and, of course, I still struggle. I have days, even weeks, where I don't love my body.

Where I find myself falling back into the belief that I will be worthy of love once I find the right diet, the right meditation routine, the right supplement. *Yes, yes,* hisses that old, familiar voice, *you must bounce back.* But I always remind myself that there is no bouncing back after having a kid; there's only bouncing forward, and the ball is different now. And it will continue to change. The key is to find peace in that flux.

That peace is hard-won, and I know how incredibly lucky I am to have the resources for it. The mental health care, the support from friends and family, the time and space to recover. Everyone deserves the same. Money might not buy happiness, but it can fund the tools and space it takes to find peace. Trauma itself doesn't make us stronger. It's the steps we take afterward. I know that I worked hard to take the right steps for me, but I am not blind to the privilege I had pushing me along. Everyone. Deserves. The. Same.

All of that is to say: I was one of many who were traumatized by the actions of Tyra and the producers. But still, I am grateful.

So, here's what I would say:

Thank you. Pay me.

ACKNOWLEDGMENTS

First things first, thank you to my daughter, Esben. I started this book when I was pregnant with you, and I never would have known how to finish it if you hadn't arrived and made my life complete. I love you so much. I wish you knew how to read.

The story began in 2007, and I'm so grateful to all of my competition, the girls (now badass women) of Cycle 9. Thank you especially to everyone who shared their stories in interviews: Kimberly (and thank you for answering my frantic texts, I love you), Ambreal, Claire, Marvita, Heather, Lisa, Sarah, Corinne, David, Oliver, and more. And to Jenah, who is always one step ahead of me.

Of course, without Ayla Zuraw-Friedland and the Francis Goldin Agency, I never would have known how to even begin, middle, or end this book. I am so grateful that you slid into my Twitter DMs all those years ago; you changed my life forever. You're my favorite manic gremlin dream girl.

I know I dedicated the book to him, but I also have to thank my husband, Ian Leue, for the hours, days, weeks, months, years of support and love. I want every writer to have a partner like you. LMWTF.

To JJ: thank you for everything. You're an extraordinary young woman, and we're so lucky Esben has you in her life.

To Pam: I have literally sent you two voice memos since I started writing this. Thank you for listening to them and for always being on my team. It's a joy and a privilege to be on yours.

To my co-producer, co-host, and biological son, Tyler Mead: thank you for picking up all the slack of our various projects when I was deep in the writing rabbit hole.

Thank you to everyone at Crown who helped make this possible but, obviously, especially Aubrey Martinson. It was an honor to work with you. Thank you for your patience, thank you for being gentle when I asked you to be, but, most important, thank you for pushing me when I needed you to. You're a stone-cold boss.

After my grandfather died, I was lost without him and his advice. Thank you to Dan Halpern and my aunt Caerthan for stepping in and fielding my calls and questions, even as we all struggled to navigate our grief.

I was lucky enough to have a chapter of this book published by Gawker before it went under, and for that I am so grateful to George Civeris for editing the piece and being a damn delight at all times.

My group chats: Bloody Merries, the Clay Mask Golems, Haters, Whisper of Peen, So You Think You Can DJ, Acid Mothers. You are the dumb, weird, beautiful, perfect threads that sew me together.

To my mom and dad: thank you for listening to all the stories that led to this one. I love you.

BIBLIOGRAPHY

Alexander, J. *Follow the Model: Miss J's Guide to Unleashing Presence, Poise, and Power*. New York: Simon Spotlight Entertainment, 2009.

Ford, Ashley C. *Somebody's Daughter: A Memoir*. New York: Flatiron Books, 2021.

Harrison, Christy. *Anti-Diet: Reclaim Your Time, Money, Well-Being, and Happiness Through Intuitive Eating*. New York: Little, Brown Spark, 2019.

Mailer, Norman. *Of Women and Their Elegance*. New York: Simon & Schuster, 1980.

Manuel, Jay. *The Wig, the Bitch & the Meltdown: The Devil Also Wears Cheap Shoes*. Beacon, NY: Wordeee, 2020.

Millwood, Molly. *To Have and to Hold: Motherhood, Marriage, and the Modern Dilemma*. New York: Harper Wave, 2019.

Montell, Amanda. *Cultish: The Language of Fanaticism*. New York: Harper Wave, 2021.

Nussbaum, Emily. *Cue the Sun! The Invention of Reality TV*. New York: Random House, 2024.

Ratajkowski, Emily. *My Body*. New York: Metropolitan Books, 2021.

Renn, Crystal. *Hungry*. New York: Simon & Schuster, 2009.

Tolentino, Jia. *Trick Mirror: Reflections on Self-Delusion*. New York: Random House, 2019.

Trow, George W. S. "Within the Context of No Context." *New Yorker*, November 9, 1980.

Valenti, Jessica. *Sex Object: A Memoir*. New York: Dey St., 2016.

SARAH HARTSHORNE is a writer, comedian, and content creator. She was the plus-size contestant on Cycle 9 of *America's Next Top Model*. After the show, she modeled all over the world for clients like *Glamour, Vogue,* Skechers, and more. She's written about her experiences with plus-size modeling, travel, and body image for *The Guardian,* Gawker, and *Teen Vogue.* She lives in New York City with her husband, daughter, and two elderly cats.